D0403855

THREE
ONE-ACT
PLAYS

WOODY ALLEN

THREE ONE-ACT PLAYS

RIVERSIDE DRIVE
OLD SAYBROOK
CENTRAL PARK WEST

RANDOM HOUSE TRADE PAPERBACKS

NEW YORK

Library of Congress Cataloging-in-Publication Data
Allen, Woody.
[Plays. Selections]
Three one-act plays / by Woody Allen.
p. cm.
Contents: Writer's block—Riverside Drive—
Old Saybrook—Central Park West.
ISBN 0-8129-7244-9 (pbk.)
I. Title.

PS3551.L44T47 2003
812'.54—dc22   2003061185

Random House website address:
www.atrandom.com

Printed in the United States of America

4   5   6   7   8   9

Book design by Pei Loi Koay

CONTENTS

WRITER'S BLOCK

RIVERSIDE DRIVE

Curtain rises on a gray day in New York. There might even be some hint of fog. The setting suggests a secluded spot by the embankment of the Hudson River where one can lean over the rail, watch the boats and see the New Jersey shoreline. Probably the West Seventies or Eighties.

Jim Swain, a writer, somewhere between forty and fifty, is waiting nervously, checking his watch, pacing, trying a number on his cellular phone to no response. He's obviously waiting to meet someone.

He rubs his hands together, checks for some drizzle and perhaps pulls his jacket up a bit as he feels at least a damp mist.

Presently, a large, homeless man, unshaven, a street dweller of approximately Jim's age, drifts on with a kind of eye on Jim. His name is Fred.

Fred eventually drifts closer to Jim, who has become increasingly aware of his presence and, while not exactly afraid, is wary of being in a desolate area with a large, unsavory type. Add to this that Jim wants his rendezvous with whomever he is waiting for to be very private. Finally, Fred engages him.

FRED
Rainy day.
(Jim nods, agreeing but not wanting to encourage conversation.)
A drizzle.
(Jim nods with a wan smile.)
Or should I say mizzle—mist and drizzle.

JIM
Um.

FRED
(pause)
Look at how fast the current's moving. You throw your cap into the river it'll be out in the open sea in twenty minutes.

JIM
(begrudging but polite)
Uh-huh . . .

FRED
(pause)
The Hudson River travels three hundred and fifteen miles beginning in the Adirondacks and emptying finally into the vast Atlantic Ocean.

JIM
Interesting.

FRED
No it's not. Ever wonder what it'd be like if the current ran in the opposite direction?

JIM
I haven't actually.

FRED
Chaos—the world would be out of sync. You throw your cap in it'd get carried up to Poughkeepsie rather than out to sea.

JIM
Yes . . . well . . .

FRED
Ever been to Poughkeepsie?

JIM
What?

FRED
Ever been to Poughkeepsie?

JIM
Me?

FRED
(looks around; they're alone)
Who else?

JIM
Why do you ask?

FRED
It's a simple question.

JIM
If I was in Poughkeepsie?

FRED
Were you?

JIM
(considers the question, decides he'll answer)
No, I haven't. OK?

FRED
So if you haven't, why are you so guilty?

JIM
Look, I'm a little preoccupied.

FRED
You don't come here often, do you?

JIM
Why?

FRED
Interesting.

JIM

What do you want? Are you going to hit me up for a touch?
Here, here's a buck.

FRED

Hey—I only asked if you came here often.

JIM
(getting impatient)
No. I'm meeting someone. I have a lot on my mind.

FRED
What a day you picked.

JIM
I didn't know it would be this nasty.

FRED
Don't you watch the weather on TV? Christ, it seems that all
they talk about is the goddamn weather. You really care on
Riverside Drive if there are gusty winds in the Appalachian
Valley? I mean, Jesus, gimme a break.

JIM
Well, it was nice talking to you.

FRED
Look—you can hardly see Jersey—there's such a fog.

JIM
It's OK. It's a blessing . . .

FRED

Right. I don't like it any better than you do.

JIM

Actually I'm joking—I'm being—

FRED

Frivolous? ... Flippant?

JIM

Mildly sarcastic.

FRED

It's understandable.

JIM

It is?

FRED

Knowing how I feel about Montclair.

JIM

How would I know how you feel about Montclair?

FRED

I won't even bother to comment on that.

JIM

Er—yeah—well—I'd like to get back to my thoughts.
(Looks at watch.)

FRED

What time you expect her?

JIM

What are you talking about? Please leave me alone.

FRED

It's a free country. I can stay here and stare at New Jersey if I
want.

JIM

Fine. But don't talk to me.

FRED

Don't answer.

JIM

(takes out cell phone)
Hey look, do you want me to call the police?

FRED

And tell them what?

JIM

That you're harassing me—aggressive panhandling.

FRED

Suppose I took that cell phone and tossed it right into the river.
Twenty minutes it'd be carried off into the Atlantic. Of course,
if the current ran the other way it'd wind up in Poughkeepsie.
Do I mean Poughkeepsie or Tarrytown?

JIM

(a bit scared and angry)
I've been to Tarrytown in case you were going to ask me that
next.

FRED

Where'd you stay there?

JIM

Pocantico Hills. I used to live there. Is that OK with you?

FRED

Now they call it Sleepy Hollow—sounds better for the tourists.

JIM

Uh-huh.

FRED

Cash in on all that Ichabod Crane crap. Rip Van Winkle. It's all packaging.

JIM

Look—I was deep in thought—

FRED

Hey—we're talking literature. You're a writer.

JIM

How do you know that?

FRED

C'mon—it's me.

JIM

Are you going to tell me you can tell because of my costume?

FRED

You're in costume?

JIM

It's the tweed jacket and the corduroys, right?

FRED

Jean-Paul Sartre said that after the age of thirty a man is responsible for his own face.

JIM

Camus said that.

FRED
Sartre.

JIM
Camus. Sartre said a man assumes the traits of his occupation—
a waiter will gradually walk like a waiter—a bank clerk
gestures like one—because they want to become things.

FRED
But you're not a thing.

JIM
I try not to be.

FRED
Because it's safe to be a thing—because things don't perish.
Like *The Wall*—the men being executed want to become one
with the wall they're put up in front of—to lose themselves in
the stone—to become solid, permanent, to endure, in other
words, to live, to be alive.

JIM
(considers him—then)
I'd love to discuss this with you another time.

FRED
Good, when?

JIM
Right now I'm a little busy . . .

FRED
Well, when? You want to have lunch, I'm free all week.

JIM
I don't really know.

FRED

I wrote a funny thing based on Irving.

JIM

Irving who?

FRED

Washington Irving—remember? We had talked about Ichabod
Crane.

JIM

I didn't know we were back on that.

FRED

The headless horseman is doomed to ride the countryside,
holding his head under his arm. He was a German soldier killed
in the war.

JIM

A Hessian.

FRED

So he rides right into an all-night drugstore and the head
says—I have a terrible headache—and the druggist says, here,
take these two Extra Strength Excedrin—and the body pays for
them and helps the head take two. And then we cut to them
later in the night, riding over a bridge, and the head says, I feel
great—the headache is gone—I'm a new man—and then the
body begins to get sad and thinks how unlucky he is because if
he gets a backache, he can't find relief, not being attached to the
head—

JIM

How can the body think anything?

FRED

Nobody's going to ask that question.

JIM

Why not? It's obvious.

FRED

That's why. That's why you're good at construction and
dialogue but you lack inspiration. That's why you have to
rely on me. Although it was a pretty sleazy thing to do.

JIM

Do what? What are you talking about?

FRED

I'm talking about money—some kind of payment and a credit
of some sort.

JIM

Look, I'm meeting someone.

FRED

I know, I know, she's late.

JIM

You don't know and mind your own business.

FRED

All right—you're meeting a broad—you want to be alone?
Let's get the business end of it out of the way and I'm off.

JIM

What business?

FRED

In a minute you're gonna tell me this whole thing is
Kafkaesque.

JIM

It's worse than Kafkaesque.

FRED
Really? Is it—postmodern?

JIM
What do you want?

FRED
A percentage and a credit on your movie. I realize it's too late
for a credit on the prints that are already in distribution, but I
should have a royalty on those and a cut and my name on all
subsequent prints. Not fifty percent but something fair.

JIM
Are you nuts? Why should I give you anything?

FRED
Because I gave you the idea.

JIM
You gave me?

FRED
Well—you took it from me—

JIM
I took your idea?

FRED
And you sold your first film script—and the movie seems like a
success and I want what's due me.

JIM
I didn't take your idea.

FRED
Jim, let's not play games.

JIM

Let's not you play games and don't call me Jim.

FRED

OK—James. Written by James L. Swain—but everyone calls you Jim.

JIM

How do you know what everyone calls me?

FRED

I see it, I hear it.

JIM

Where? What are you talking about?

FRED

Jim Swain—Central Park West and Seventy-eighth—BMW—license plate JIMBO ONE—talk about vanity plates . . . Jimmy Connors is Jimbo One, not you—and I've seen you trying to hit a tennis ball so don't try and con me.

JIM

Have you been following me?

FRED

That mousey brunette—that's Lola?

JIM

My wife's hardly mousey!

FRED

OK, "mousey" was the wrong word—she's—not rodentine exactly—

JIM

She's a beautiful woman.

FRED
It's all very subjective.

JIM
Who the hell do you think you are?

FRED
I'd never say it to her face.

JIM
I'm her husband and I love her.

FRED
Then why are you cheating?

JIM
What?

FRED
I think I know what the other one looks like. She's a little on the cheap side, no?

JIM
There is no other one.

FRED
Then who are you meeting?

JIM
None of your goddamn business, and if you don't get out of here I'm going to call the police.

FRED
That's the last thing you want if you're having a clandestine rendezvous.

JIM

How did you know my wife's name is Lola?

FRED

I've heard you call her Lola.

JIM

Have you been stalking me?

FRED

Do I look like a stalker?

JIM

Yes.

FRED

I'm a writer. At least I was years ago. Till my visions
overtook me.

JIM

Well, your imagination is too creative for me.

FRED

I know. That's why you ripped me off.

JIM

I didn't steal your idea.

FRED

Not just my idea. It was autobiographical. So in a way you
stole my life.

JIM

If there were any similarities between my film and your life, I
assure you, they're coincidental.

FRED

I'm not the kind of guy who sues. Some people are litigation-prone.
(with some suggestion of menace)
I like to settle between the parties.

JIM

How did I take your idea?

FRED

You overheard me tell the plot.

JIM

To who? Where?

FRED

Central Park.

JIM

I heard you in Central Park?

FRED

That's right.

JIM

To who? When?

FRED

To John.

JIM

Who?

FRED

John.

JIM
John who?

FRED
Big John.

JIM
Who?

FRED
Big John.

JIM
Who the hell is Big John?

FRED
I don't know—he's a homeless guy. Was. I heard he got his throat cut in a shelter.

JIM
You told some tale to a homeless man and you're saying I overheard you?

FRED
And used it.

JIM
I never saw you in my life.

FRED
Christ, I've been stalking you for months.

JIM
Stalking me?

FRED

And I know everything about you but you never even noticed me. And I'm not a little guy. I'm big. I could probably snap your neck in half with one hand.

JIM
(nervous)
Look—whoever you are, I promise—

FRED

The name's Fred. Fred Savage. Good name for a writer, isn't it? For Best Original Screenplay, the envelope please—and the winners are Frederick R. Savage and James L. Swain for *The Journey*.

JIM

I wrote *The Journey*. And it was my idea.

FRED

Jim, you overheard me telling it to John Kelly. Poor John. He was walking on York Avenue and they were hoisting a piano and the rope came undone—God, it was awful . . .

JIM

You said he was knifed at a shelter.

FRED

Foolish consistency is the hobgoblin of small minds.

JIM

Look, Fred—I never stole anybody's idea. First, I don't need to because I have my own ideas, and second, I wouldn't even if I ran dry, OK?

FRED

But the story's all there. My breakdown, the straitjacket, my last-minute panic—the rubber between my teeth, then the electric shocks—my God—of course I was violent—

JIM

You're violent?

FRED

In and out.

JIM

Look, I'm starting to get a little alarmed.

FRED

Don't worry, she'll be here.

JIM

Over you, not her. OK—if you think you're a writer—

FRED

I said years ago—before my collapse—before all that unpleasantness occurred—I wrote for an agency.

JIM

Unpleasantness?

FRED

It's morbid, I don't want to relive it.

JIM

What kind of an agency?

FRED

An ad agency. I wrote commercials. Like that idea for the Extra Strength Excedrin one. It didn't fly. We ran it up the flagpole but it just didn't fly. Too Cartesian.

JIM
And you became—unhinged.

FRED
Not over that. Who cares that they reject my idea? Those gray flannel philistines. No, my problem arose from other sources.

JIM
Like what?

FRED
Like small cadres of men who had banded together to form a conspiratorial network—a network dedicated to my undoing, to my humiliation, to my defeat both physical and mental. A network so vast and complex that to this day it employs undercover agents in organizations as diverse as the CIA and the Cuban underground. Forces so malevolent that they cost me my job, my marriage, and what little bank account I had left. They trailed me, tapped my phone, and communicated in code with my psychiatrist by sending electrical signals from the top of the Empire State Building, through my inner ear, directly to his rubber raft at Martha's Vineyard. So don't give me your goddamn sob stories and deal with me like a mensch!

JIM
I'm frightened, Fred—I gotta level with you. I want to do the right thing by you—

FRED
Then do it. There's no need to be scared. I haven't been off my medicine long enough to lose control—at least I don't think I have—

JIM
What do you take?

FRED

A number of antipsychotic mixtures.

JIM

A cocktail.

FRED

Except I don't drink it out of a stemmed glass.

JIM

But you can't just go off those things—

FRED

I'm fine, I'm fine. Don't start accusing me like the others.

JIM

No, I'm not—

FRED

Let's talk turkey.

JIM

I had intended to prove to you logically I couldn't have taken your idea—

FRED

My life, my life—you stole my life.

JIM

Your life—your autobiography, whatever. I think I can show you step by step—

FRED

Logic can be very deceptive. You stole my life, you stole my soul.

JIM

I don't need your life. I have a fine life of my own.

FRED

Who are you to say you don't need my life?

JIM

I didn't mean to insult you.

FRED

Look, I realize you're under personal strain.

JIM

I am, yes.

FRED

And she's quite late—that's a bad sign.

JIM

I'm surprised. She's usually punctual.

FRED

She must sense something's up. I'd keep alert if I was you.

JIM

I am. I just want to point out that my film—

FRED

Our film—

JIM

The film—is it OK if I say *the* film? *The* film is about the evils of one particular mental institution which I happened to set in New Jersey.

FRED

Been there, done that.

JIM

But surely many people had similar experiences. This could be their story as easily.

FRED

No—no—you heard me tell it. I even said to Big John Kelly it would make a swell film—especially the part where the protagonist lights the fires.

JIM

Is that what happened in your life?

FRED

You know the details.

JIM

I swear I don't.

FRED

I was under instructions to burn down several buildings.

JIM

Instructions, from who?

FRED

The radio.

JIM

You heard voices over the radio?

FRED

Do I hear the barest trace of skepticism in your voice?

JIM

No—

FRED

I was not always—whatever was their term—

JIM

Paranoid schizophrenic?

FRED

What'd you say?

JIM

I was trying to be helpful.

FRED

Everyone's so damn technical. That's all semantics. It used to be dementia praecox—actually that's prettier. It's worse than semantics, it's cosmetics. A girl brings her fiance home to meet her parents and says, folks, this is Max, he's a manic-depressive. You can imagine how they take it. Fantasies of their darling child wed to a guy who on Monday tries to jump off the Chrysler Building and Tuesday tries to buy every item in Bloomingdale's—ah, but say, this is Max—he's bipolar. It sounds like an achievement—like an explorer—bipolar like Admiral Byrd.

No, Jim—they diagnosed me in more prosaic terms. Not screwy or off his rocker—we're not talking vaudeville here—they said Fred Savage is homicidal—an unpredictable psychopath.

JIM

Homicidal?

FRED

Don't you just love labels?

JIM

Er—look, Fred, aware as you are of being delusional you can then see why I might think your theory, that I took your idea, may not be based on reality.

FRED

Who's to say what's real? Are we particles or rays? Is everything expanding or contracting? If we enter a black hole and the laws of physics are suspended, will I still need an athletic supporter?

JIM

Fred, you're obviously an educated man—

FRED

Phi Beta Kappa. Brown University. I can read Sanskrit. Ph.D. in Literature. Dissertation on the Positive Results of the Triangular Tension Between Goethe, Schopenhauer and Schopenhauer's Mother. So what was I doing in an ad agency, you ask? Having nervous breakdowns—not just because the hacks failed to see the brilliance of my Extra Strength Excedrin concept but because they were blind to the originality of my thought in general. Example: eight whores are sitting around in a brothel. A john comes in and surveys them up and down. He finally passes them all up and selects the umbrella stand in the corner. He goes down the hall with it in his arms, takes it to bed and has intense and passionate sexual intercourse with it. Cut to him driving off in a VW Beetle and we flash on the screen— Volkswagen—for the man with special taste. God, how they hated that one.

By now I was in and out of institutions like I had a season ticket. And when I lost my job, my girlfriend, Henrietta, who I believe only put up with me because she had a severe disorder of her own, which might charitably be characterized as thermonuclear masochism, kicked me out.

Yes, Jim—I was very upset. I wept. Salty tears descended

these rubicund cheeks—and in an effort to woo her back I went searching for an appropriate offering with which to hopefully mollify her newly discovered feelings of disgust for me. Aware of her taste for antique jewelry I surmised an old pin or Victorian brooch might turn the trick, and having selected just the right one in a Third Avenue antique shop, I by chance came across a very stylish 1940s radio, perfect for my kitchen. Red plastic it was—a Philco. And when I got it home and tried it out, I was surprised to hear an announcer's voice commanding me to burn down the very ad agency I had formerly worked for. It was the most fun I've ever had. Am I losing you?

JIM
This is a very sad story.

FRED
I loved that girl, Henrietta. And while her attention deficit disorder made any conversation between us longer than forty seconds impossible, something in our contact buoyed my spirits. That's why I can empathize with your pathetic love life.

JIM
My love life is just fine.

FRED
Jim—you're talking to your writing partner.

JIM
You're not my writing partner.

FRED
You need a collaborator.

JIM
I've never collaborated in my life.

FRED

You're good at the nuts and bolts—but you need someone who can light a fire. I'm an idea man. OK, some may be a little avant-garde for Mr. and Mrs. Front Porch.

JIM

I have my own ideas.

FRED

If you did you wouldn't have swiped mine.

JIM

I didn't swipe it.

FRED

Genius is in the chromosomes. Did you know my personal DNA glows in the dark?

JIM

What makes you think I'm so uninspired?

FRED

I think you're very—professional. It's very solid—notice you do a lot of adaptations—not originals—I, on the other hand, am a true original—like Stravinsky—or ketchup. That's why my idea was the first thing you ever did that meant anything. It had juice—it had spark.

JIM

I thought of it in the shower.

FRED
(turning on him violently)
Don't give me that jive! I want my half!

JIM

For Christ's sake, stay calm.

FRED

And don't tell me your love life's fine. Because what the hell
are you doing sneaking around on Lola?

JIM

That's not your affair.

FRED

No, it's your affair.

JIM

I'm not having an affair.

FRED

What's wrong with Lola?

JIM

Nothing.

FRED

Apart from a certain—what is it I mean—is it a ferret?

JIM

Keep your mouth shut. You're talking about the woman I love.

FRED

What's wrong there?

JIM

Nothing.

FRED

Jim.

JIM

Nothing.

FRED
Jim, c'mon.

JIM
It was fine till we had the twins.

FRED
Right—two perfect look-alikes—a grizzly omen.

JIM
They're adorable boys.

FRED
Boys—at least twin girls you can dress cute.

JIM
They're cute—they're cuddly—they're—

FRED
Exactly identical?

JIM
So what?

FRED
And they both have Lola's gerbil-like visage?

JIM
Before they came we had a perfectly good marriage.

FRED
Says who?

JIM
I'm telling you, it was fine.

FRED

Just fine? Not great?

JIM

We shared a lot of interests.

FRED

Name two.

JIM

Weekends in Connecticut and macrobiotic food.

FRED

I'm falling asleep here.

JIM

We liked to scuba dive and discuss the great books.

FRED

You discussed books underwater?

JIM

And she plays piano and I play baritone sax.

FRED

Thank God it's not the other way around.

JIM

Go ahead—make fun of me.

FRED

What about your sex life?

JIM

That's none of your business.

FRED
Those two big front teeth of hers—do they hurt?

JIM
Why must you be a vulgar smart-ass?

FRED
I'm trying to grasp your situation. How often did you make love?

JIM
Often. Till the twins were born.

FRED
I'd say you were basically a missionary position man, am I right?

JIM
(annoyed)
We did our share of experimenting.

FRED
What do you call experimenting?

JIM
Why must you know?

FRED
We're a team.

JIM
(annoyed)
That's right.
(slight pause)
We had a threesome once, OK?

FRED
Who was the other woman?

JIM
It was a guy.

FRED
Are you bisexual?

JIM
I never touched him.

FRED
Whose idea was the threesome?

JIM
Hers.

FRED
I wonder why.

JIM
We'd seen it on the porn channel one night.

FRED
You watch that consistently?

JIM
Of course not. But sometimes you can get some good ideas.

FRED
Aha—so you do use other people's ideas.

JIM
And once we did it at her parents' house during the
Thanksgiving dinner.

FRED

Did the other dinner guests look up from their turkey?

JIM

We were in the bathroom!

FRED

So there was a certain spontaneity.

JIM

I don't know why you think I'm so lackluster.

FRED

Did Lola have an orgasm?

JIM

I don't think I'll dignify that with an answer.

FRED

They have been known to fake it, you know.

JIM

Why on earth would she fake it?

FRED

Bolster your confidence. She doesn't want you to know you're not satisfying her.

JIM

I'm completely secure about my sexual prowess.

FRED

You know what they say.

JIM

What?

FRED

A dog doesn't see its own tail.

JIM

What the hell does that mean?

FRED

Maybe you think you're better than you are.

JIM

That's not true.

FRED

Then why would Lola fake it?

JIM

You said she faked it.

FRED

That's the message I'm getting.

JIM

What message?

FRED

From the top of the Empire State Building. I'm feeling those rays—those electrical charges from the big antenna on the Empire State Building and all those photons are saying—Lola was pretending to come.

JIM

Hey look, I'm trying to have a rational—

FRED

And then came the twins—David and Seth.

JIM

Carson and Django.

FRED

Really?

JIM

Lola's a big fan of Carson McCullers—

FRED

And you play jazz so—

JIM

So they *weren't* conventional names.

FRED

And you love them.

JIM

I'm crazy about them. But Lola's too crazy about them.
Suddenly everything changed—it all became about the twins—
there was never any time for me anymore—for us.

FRED

No more underwater discussions of Proust.

JIM

Naturally the sex fell off.

FRED

And you started cheating.

JIM

Yes—yes—

FRED

Hmmm . . . that explains a lot. Look—take my advice, call it quits with your mistress—it can only lead to heartache.

JIM

I don't need your advice. That's what I planned to do today. If she ever gets here.

FRED

Maybe she senses you want it over so she's not coming.

JIM

She doesn't have a clue. She'll be stunned.

FRED

Oh great, I think I'll stick around and watch this.

JIM

What the hell am I doing having an affair? Six lousy months of dark restaurants, dingy bars, and cheap hotel rooms. Not to mention the furtive phone calls and the tension and self-hate.

FRED

What does your psychiatrist say?

JIM

He said stop.

FRED

And you—

JIM

I stopped—seeing the psychiatrist.

FRED

It's just as well, most of them have hidden tape recorders.

JIM

Last night I came home and I saw Lola sitting on the sofa, curled up like—like—

FRED

A tiny guinea pig?

JIM

I wasn't going to say that. Like a sweet, decent woman who's been my closest friend my whole life.

FRED

Did you ever lead this woman on? Make any promises, tell her you loved her or that you might leave your wife?

JIM

Absolutely not—in no way—not for a second.

FRED

I don't know why, but I'm sensing a vibration that says maybe you did.

JIM

That's nonsense.

FRED

Um, I don't know . . .

JIM

She wanted me to go to the Caribbean with her—for five days. I was to lie to Lola and say it was a business trip.

FRED

And you agreed?

JIM

Not exactly—I said I'd think about it. It was a moment of weakness. Our clothes were off and I'd had three margaritas and there was so much salt on the rim of the glasses and I'm on a salt-free diet . . . So I suddenly got a sodium rush.

FRED

(folding paws downward in front of him, mimicking Lola)
But when you got home and saw your precious darling . . .

JIM

Exactly—it was at the moment I was supposed to lie that I knew that I loved Lola despite all our problems and I was a fool.

FRED

This could get ugly.

JIM

Nothing's getting ugly. She's an adult and I'm an adult.

FRED

You said she was headstrong.

JIM

I never said any such thing.

FRED

I heard some voice say it, I *thought* it was yours.

JIM

Look, these things happen. People break off their affairs every day—don't they?

FRED

So that's why you picked such a secluded spot—you're anticipating a scene.

JIM

Hey look—why am I discussing women with you? Your view
of everything is skewed.

FRED

I was married once.

JIM

You were?

FRED

I don't remember much about it—all that AC/DC through my
head plays havoc with your memory but I do recall she was
forever dialing 911.

JIM

You know what? Here's what I think—

FRED

Come in.

JIM

I think you should just leave and get back on your medicine.
I'm not fooling—I'd say megadoses if possible—I don't want
you around here when she comes, I can manage by myself.

FRED

OK, fine. Then let's settle our business and I'm history.

JIM

What business? We have no business. I didn't steal your idea.

FRED

Maybe on the next one you could make it up to me with an
adjusted fee and top billing.

JIM
There is no next one. I don't collaborate. I work alone. I—oh—
(notices Barbara approaching)
Oh oh . . . oh . . . oh . . . walk away . . . go, go . . .

FRED
You're all white.

JIM
She's coming.

FRED
All right, don't panic.

JIM
You got me so distracted.

FRED
All I said was I think you're in for rough going.

JIM
Why do you say that?

FRED
Empire State Building.

JIM
No, it's going to be fine. I practiced my speech in the shower. I
was in there an hour and a half. I know exactly what I'm going
to say. Get out of here!
(Barbara is there now.)

BARBARA
Sorry I'm late. Who's this?

JIM
Oh—I don't know . . .
(Jim gesturing with his head, trying to signal Fred to leave.)

BARBARA
Are you having a neck spasm?

JIM
(hands Fred money)
Er—here's the buck you asked for, fella, go get a square meal—
good luck, buddy . . . ha, ha . . .

FRED
Fred. Fred Savage. I'm a friend of Jim's.

BARBARA
You didn't say anything—

JIM
He's kidding.

FRED
I'm his writing partner.

BARBARA
Writing partner?

FRED
We collaborated on *The Journey*—it was my idea—he did the
actual screenplay.
(calling off)
Come in.

BARBARA
What? What's going on?

FRED
Tell her, Jim.

BARBARA
Tell me what?

JIM
Fred—leave us alone.

FRED
I'm afraid you'll pussyfoot.

BARBARA
Jim, is something wrong?

FRED
The best way is to be direct.

JIM
Get out of here, Fred.

FRED
Barbara, Jim has something to tell you.

BARBARA
About what? What is this?

FRED
About your extramarital affair.

JIM
Fred's crazy—he's a street lunatic.

FRED
Tell her, Jim, or I will.

BARBARA
What's going on here?

JIM
This is none of your business.

BARBARA
I didn't know you had a writing partner.

JIM
I don't.

FRED
I'm the idea man, Jim handles the construction and dialogue.
Although I'm not bad at dialogue. I wrote a great copy line
once for these wonderful Japanese air conditioners—

JIM
Fred—

FRED
"They're sleek, they're silent, they'll freeze your ass off."
Company would not go for it.

JIM
Let's go someplace where we can be alone.

FRED
He can't go to the Caribbean, Barbara—too attached to his wife.

BARBARA
Jim—

FRED
He wanted to tell Lola but when it came time to confront her
the boy lost his resolve.

BARBARA

I don't believe this.

JIM

Barbara, try and understand.

BARBARA

Is this true? Is everything off?

JIM

I can't do it, Barbara, I've made a decision.

BARBARA

One minute you're all over me, making plans, talking big—

JIM

It was your idea. I never wanted to go away.

BARBARA

So you're through using me and now it's back to Lola.

JIM

I wasn't using you. We both knew what we were doing every step of the way.

BARBARA

You think you can just manipulate me like one of those characters in your scripts?

JIM

I sensed it was becoming too hot and heavy, so before it got totally out of control—

BARBARA

I'm sorry, Jim—it is out of control. I want to talk to Lola.

JIM
Talk to Lola?

BARBARA
Yes. I think once she hears it from me she'll get the picture.
(Pauses, looks around hopelessly.)

JIM
(calling off)
Come in.

BARBARA
I don't believe you love her more than me. I'm going to meet
with her and have this out.

JIM
(to Fred)
Say something, you're my collaborator!

FRED
I'm just the idea man, you do the dialogue.

JIM
I need a fresh concept.

FRED
Look, Barbara—may I call you Barbara?

BARBARA
I don't know who the hell you are but take a hike.

FRED
My name is Frederick R. Savage and although it does not
appear on the screen or the products, I coauthored Jim's first
movie and am also the inventor of the cordless phone and
instant coffee.

JIM
Fred—for Christ's sake!

FRED
(calling off)
Yes? Come in.

BARBARA
Promises were made to me.

JIM
Never—just the opposite—

FRED
Try and empathize, Barbara—a weak individual—a domestic crisis—a sexual impasse—suddenly an alluring creature such as yourself—the boy is of course swept away—he has fantasies, he gets lost—then one night he sees his family and is overcome by a flood of memories—guilt pervades his every pore—that same night a small spacecraft from the star Vega sends out magnetic rays which lodge inside his skull—

JIM
Fred, you're not helping me.

BARBARA
I'm sorry, Jim—it wasn't Lola you were thinking of all those nights we were locked in each other's arms.

JIM
You misread the situation—or I did—I've made a terrible mistake, I'd like to undo it—

BARBARA
I'm all shaken up—I have to rethink my plans. One thing is for certain though—I'm not some patsy who's going to roll over and play dead. You're gonna have to make this up to me somehow.

JIM
What does that mean?

BARBARA
I need time to think—but you're not walking out of this
scot-free. You know what they say—if you can't get love,
get money.

JIM
That's blackmail.

BARBARA
You should've thought of that when you first checked us into
that fleabag hotel—now I'm calling the shots. You'll hear from
me.
(Barbara exits.)

FRED
I know what you're thinking—it all worked so great in the
shower.

JIM
Fred—Fred—what do I do?

FRED
One thing is for sure—you can't pay her anything.

JIM
No?

FRED
You'd never be rid of her—she'd come back for more and
more—she'd bleed you white—your kids might even have
to go to public school.

JIM
I have to tell Lola—I have to—it's the only way—

FRED
It is?

JIM
It's better coming from me than from a malicious stranger.

FRED
Really?

JIM
Plus it puts an end to her threat of blackmail.

FRED
You can't tell Lola you've been having an affair for six months.

JIM
Why not? If I bring her flowers—

FRED
There's not enough flowers in the Botanical Gardens.

JIM
People have affairs and then realize they did wrong.

FRED
You're being too rational. Lola's got zero tolerance for infidelity.
It was the bane of her childhood.

JIM
How do you know?

FRED
My dog told me.

JIM
I'll tell her it meant nothing. A little sexual fling.

FRED

Great. Wives love to hear that—she'll smile warmly and then serve you with papers.

JIM

What if I denied it? It'd be my word against some hysterical stranger. Who'd Lola believe?

FRED

Come in!

JIM

I'm dead—it's over. There is no way out of this. I sinned and I'm going to hell.

FRED

Hold on a second—I'm starting to pick up a radio signal . . . I feel the rays entering my head.

JIM

I don't need rays—I need a creative idea. For Christ's sake, we're both writers—

FRED

So much damn static . . .

JIM

Unless I just pay her off.

FRED

This weather is bad for transmission.

JIM

What have I done? The sins of the father are visited on the children.

FRED
It's so annoying.

JIM
We could move—get a motor home—we could travel around—
she'd never find us.

FRED
Someone must be cooking with a microwave.

JIM
No, that's not going to work—I'm damned no matter what I do.

FRED
Wait, wait—got it! Got it!

JIM
Got what, Fred?

FRED
The solution to your problem has registered on my cortex on
Gamma Channel 2000.

JIM
Great—my head doesn't get cable.

FRED
You have to get rid of her.

JIM
Uh-huh—that's your insight?

FRED
No. I mean, get rid of her definitively.

JIM
What do you mean?

FRED

My voice says, permanent elimination.

JIM

Fine—but how, short of killing her? I can't think of any other
way—I—
(realizes that's what Fred means)
Fred—I'm trying to have a serious discussion here.

FRED

I'm very serious.

JIM

What serious? Kill her?

FRED

It's the only way you can keep your family from coming apart.

JIM

You've been off your medication too long.

FRED

I'm getting a green signal which is the go-ahead.

JIM

Fred, I'm not going to kill her.

FRED

No?

JIM

It's psychotic—you're a psychotic.

FRED

And you're just neurotic—so there's a lot I can teach you. I
outrank you.

JIM

It's no solution—and if it was a solution I couldn't do it and if I could do it, I wouldn't do it.

FRED

Why not? It's a stroke of creative genius.

JIM

It's psychologically, morally, and intellectually wrong. It's madness.

FRED

It's a leap into the unthinkable.

JIM

Let it remain unthought.

FRED

The question is how to best do it.

JIM

That's not the question.

FRED

I wouldn't want you to get caught. New York has the death penalty now. I don't think it would help your cause much to be on the receiving end of one of those lethal injections.

JIM

No, I'd like to avoid that too. Fred—

FRED

We've got to act fast. This woman is an alien—she may even be computerized.

JIM

I don't want to discuss this.

FRED

If you don't give in to all her demands she'll tell Lola every
detail. Lola loves you, trusts you—so she had a little
postpartum obsession with the twins—I'm sure it'll pass
and you'll be back having sex every Thanksgiving.

JIM

It's too radical—you're too radical.

FRED

And you're too reasonable. See, when all avenues lead to a dead
end, I make the leap.

JIM

Yes—you make the leap but I get the injection.

FRED

You won't get caught. We'll plan it perfectly.

JIM

Caught or not, I don't want to do it. It's wrong. Thou Shalt Not
Kill.

FRED

What is that, from one of your yuppie books on etiquette?

JIM

I gotta go home.

FRED

You're not going to have a home after tomorrow.

JIM

How could I have not seen that she'd be capable of this?

FRED

Because you're a lamb—a sweet middle-class lamb *with no imagination*.

JIM

I betrayed my wife.

FRED

That's right. Not to mention the effect of divorce on innocent kids. Twins yet—as if each doesn't have enough trouble going through life with an exact duplicate.

JIM

But killing her is out of the question.

FRED

How else are you going to stop her from telling Lola? How else?

JIM

I don't know—I got such a migraine.

FRED

Try acupuncture. But don't let them put the needles too close to the medulla, that's what they did with me.

JIM

Fred, please.

FRED

Where does she live?

JIM

Near Columbia. Fred—

FRED

Apartment house? Is there a doorman who'd recognize you?

JIM
Yes, there is.

FRED
What floor?

JIM
Eleven.

FRED
What about an elevator operator?

JIM
No—just a doorman.

FRED
Twenty-four hours? Probably not—

JIM
The doorman takes a break every now and then to get coffee.

FRED
If you take the back stairs . . .

JIM
He's only away about ten minutes. It's not enough time to take
the stairs eleven flights, kill her and come down before he gets
back.

FRED
Did she tell anyone about your affair? A friend?

JIM
It was our secret. That I know.

FRED
You'd have to stop off and buy gloves.

JIM

Naturally. All I need's my prints all over the place—I—Fred, what are we talking about here?! I'm not going to kill her.

FRED

You have to, old buddy. It's either that or bye-bye Lola and the kids.

JIM

But it's inhuman. What, I sneak up to her place?

FRED

Right.

JIM

Ring the bell.

FRED

She'll be expecting you. You'll have phoned first.

JIM

And what, strangle her?

FRED

What would you like to do, it's your choice. Strangle, smother, kitchen knife . . .

JIM

Telephone wire around the neck?

FRED

If you prefer.

JIM

Or plastic bag over the head.

FRED

Make it look like a suicide—or a robbery.

JIM

That's right—I could forge a note or better yet, get her to write one using some clever ruse. She recently lost her job at a magazine. A woman alone, depressed.

FRED

Y'know what I'm thinking—if you can get some blood that's her type, you buy a gun and bullets, you take pliers and pull the lead out of one of the bullets—you freeze her blood into a slug and force it into the cartridge shell—you enter her apartment, shoot her once in the chest—she's killed with a bullet of frozen blood—it melts in her system—same type— the cops find her dead but there's no bullet to be found. Just a hole in her body with no exit wound.
(calling off)
Come in.

JIM

I could drop some item in the street, get a stranger to pick it up, get his fingerprints on it. Then I could take her to one of our hotels, check in as Sam and Felicity Arbogast, kill her in the room, leave the item and sneak down the fire staircase.

FRED

I don't like the name Felicity—it's too offbeat.

JIM

It's an easy switch. Jane Arbogast.

FRED

Plus you'd be leaving a paper trail. They got these handwriting experts.

JIM

I can sign the register with my left hand.

FRED

Wait a minute—wait a minute—no, it'd never work.

JIM

What?

FRED

I was thinking if you locked her in the closet and ran a rubber tube through the keyhole and sucked the air out.

JIM

I read a story once where the guy beat someone to death with a leg of lamb and then ate the murder weapon. That is a funny one.
(laughs)
He ate the weapon.

FRED

This is no joking matter, Jim. You're going to have to eliminate that woman and soon.

JIM

I'm not doing it, Fred. I can't.

FRED

Maybe in the end the best thing would be to call her to meet for a drink, kill her on a dark street, rob her—make it look like a mugging.

JIM

I won't do it.

FRED

On the other hand, maybe you really want your marriage to break up.

JIM

What are you saying?

FRED

Yes—get that hamster of a wife off your back and be rid of
those eerie look-alike sons and all the while you can keep
insisting you didn't dump *them*. It was out of your control—
a jealous woman wrecked your home.

JIM

Please spare me those pseudo-Freudian insights.

FRED

Of course—you wind up a free man. A divorceé—a new life—
actresses, models, discos.

JIM

That's enough.

FRED

Am I hitting on a truth?

JIM

Look, I'm not saying I'm not in a terrible predicament. I'm not
saying I wouldn't be lucky if Barbara was—was—

FRED

You can say it.

JIM

Deceased. But she's a human being.

FRED

You say that like it's a good thing.

JIM

Isn't it?

FRED

I don't know. Have you ever gone to a tenants' meeting in a co-op?

JIM

Maybe I led her on without intending to. It's possible. I may be more responsible than I realize.

FRED

But you acted out of bumbling stupidity. You're starved for a little attention at home, a little passion, so you blunder into an affair where you get some pampering and some illicit sex and you go with it. Eventually you come to your senses but it's too late. A scheming woman won't let go. You're pathetic. But that's OK, most people are pathetic. See, now, I, on the other hand, am tragic.

JIM

I'm pathetic and you're tragic?

FRED

Oh yeah. I had greatness in me. A different roll of the dice and I could have been Shakespeare or Milton.

JIM

Are you kidding? With the eight whores and a Volkswagen?

FRED

You have a chance to redeem yourself. To prevent the destruction of your family by a vindictive bitch whose rage at not getting what she wants decays into blackmail.

JIM

It's morally unacceptable.

FRED

What you've done is already morally unacceptable. You've cheated on your wife, you've lied, you've broken your marriage vows.

JIM

OK—it was wrong—but it's not murder.

FRED

You say murder like it was the ultimate act. To a more creative mind like mine it's—another option.

JIM

That's the difference between us, Fred. You have delusions of grandeur. I'm more earthbound. I don't get my instructions from rays coming from the Empire State Building or a hovering spacecraft.

FRED

That can be changed—I know a brain surgeon who can install a dish.

JIM

I accept the Judeo-Christian ethic.

FRED

You take your orders from a cartel?

JIM

You equate psychosis with creativity.

FRED

Hey, don't believe me—check your reviews over the years. What do you think the critics mean when they euphemistically refer to you as a "fine craftsman"?

JIM

That I'm a solid professional. You're just unstructured madness.

FRED

That's why we'd make a good team.

JIM

No, I don't want to be a team.

FRED

You're afraid.

JIM

Maybe—but it's my choice and I'm saying no to murder. I realize there's probably going to be very painful consequences, but I'm responsible for what I've gotten myself into and if Barbara chooses to behave like a vicious snake, taking her life is still absolutely unacceptable.

FRED

We have hit on the kernel of your problem, kid. You can't make the leap.
(Now Barbara appears on the scene again.)

BARBARA

I want to talk to you.

JIM

Barbara—I thought—

BARBARA

I'm glad you're still here.

FRED

Barbara, are you allergic to any insect sprays or roach powder?

JIM
Fred!

BARBARA
I want to speak to him alone.

FRED
Alone? How is that possible?

BARBARA
Without you around.

FRED
But we're partners.

JIM
OK, Fred—give me some space—we're not joined at the hip.

FRED
But our collaboration—

JIM
Please—I need some time with Barbara. Go chat with the
mother ship.

FRED
OK—suit yourself. I'm out of here.
(sotto to Jim)
You see that glowing red aura around her? The only time I've
ever seen it before was around Nixon.
(Fred exits.)

JIM
Barbara, I'm sorry about everything.

BARBARA
I needed a few minutes to clear my head.

JIM

You were pretty frazzled back there.

BARBARA

Everything took me by surprise.

JIM

I apologize for that. There's no easy way to end an affair.

BARBARA

I knew what I was getting myself into.

JIM

I never led you on. We're both adults.

BARBARA

I've been a little tense lately. Lost my job—been drinking a little too much.

JIM

I understand. I was going through a bad period in my marriage for a while. Maybe it'll never right itself, but having an affair is not the way I should be dealing with it. If there's anything I can do for you—

BARBARA

I'd like three hundred thousand dollars.

JIM

Just let me know.

BARBARA

Three hundred down and two more by the end of the year.

JIM

Pardon me?

BARBARA

You've come into some dough with your screenplay. I think you can manage a half mil.

JIM

Barbara, think what you're doing—

BARBARA

You think. I could make your life miserable but I'm not. That's got to be worth something.

JIM

A half million dollars—

BARBARA

You gonna quibble? I'll go to Lola right now.

JIM

I can't pay that kind of money.

BARBARA

You mean you won't.

JIM

No, I won't. Even if I could I wouldn't. Because it wouldn't stop there. You'd be all over me next year and the year after that.

BARBARA

Jim, you're not in a position to make the rules.

JIM

I'm trying to clean up a mess I made, not get deeper into it. This would tie us together forever. You'd bleed me white over the years. I'd never be free of you.

BARBARA

I want the money by tomorrow—the first payment, that is. You have twenty-four hours.

JIM

I don't need twenty-four hours.

BARBARA

If I don't hear from you by tomorrow afternoon I'll assume you'd prefer I blew the whistle. Your choice. Sleep well.
(As she goes off, Jim doesn't know where to turn, then he takes out his cellular phone.)

JIM
(ranting)
No—you won't blow any whistle because I will. I'll tell Lola myself. I'll confess everything. I'll beg her to understand. I'll weep, I'll grovel. Lola's a decent human. Maybe she can find it in her heart to forgive me . . . all right, that's a long shot . . . but I couldn't go on living knowing there was someone out there who could wreck my home on a whim . . . every time she wanted more money . . . and the payments would get bigger . . . bigger and more frequent . . . How would I explain that? No, Lola, we can't afford the apartment anymore—but I can't tell you why . . . And the vacation's out—and the boys have to get jobs. Little twin jobs . . .
(Fred has entered laconically and just observes Jim, who doesn't see Fred and speaks into the phone.)
Hello—Lola, it's Jim. Jim Swain . . . your—your husband . . . old Jim Swain, James Swain, ha, ha . . . So how've you been? Good—life treating you right? Ha, ha—what? No—I haven't been drinking. I just wanted to chat. You know I love you . . . ha, ha . . . Lola—I have something to tell you—
(Fred takes the cellular phone away and throws it onto the ground.)

FRED
What are you doing?

JIM
What'd you do?

FRED
You weren't going to confess everything to Lola, were you?

JIM
Yes I was—do you know that you were right about Barbara—
she has a red aura around her—I'm sure I saw it—she wants
five hundred thousand dollars—for openers—can you believe
that? Three hundred big ones tomorrow and the rest by the
end of the year. But I'm not paying it—not a nickel—not a
red cent.

FRED
Not to worry. Twenty minutes and Barbara'll be in the
Atlantic—or Poughkeepsie if the current ran upstream.

JIM
You don't understand, I—Fred—you didn't—

FRED
I was right about her, Jim, she takes her orders from another
galaxy.

JIM
Fred, say it isn't so—

FRED
Don't worry—there's no way you can be linked to it.

JIM
Ohmigod.

FRED

Very clever. She had a computer chip implanted in her ear. She was part of a plan to enslave the Bronx.

JIM

I've got to get out of here.

FRED

If she's ever found, somewhere in the vast Atlantic—it'll look like a suicide—they'll never know one way or the other. You said yourself, a woman alone, recently lost her job.

JIM

You threw her in the Hudson River?

FRED

All that elaborate planning—it was bad writing. The best plots are the simplest. I was sitting on a bench, she walked by—we were both alone—it came to me in a moment of inspiration. That's the difference between us two—with you it would have been labored and overanalyzed. This is not real, that's not logical. To me it just *felt* right.

JIM

I'm going to be sick.

FRED

Hey look, forget about the royalties from our movie—and forget about collaborating—truth is, I don't really want to be a writer—I'd forgotten how tedious it is—it's lonely work, Jim— and I've had an offer to be part of the next Apollo team— they're talking about a manned mission to Alpha Centauri. But keep at your work—you're a good professional—although I would recommend eventually you find someone to team up with—there's no shame in collaborating—it's just that you're missing a part.

JIM
I'm in a state of shock.

FRED
Keep your eye on the stars, Jim. There's life on many of
them—not that they necessarily mean us well. The object
of the Apollo mission is to explore some of the trouble spots
in the universe and deal with any eventuality that may occur—
the President knows about it—we've discussed it at length . . .
it's not all a bed of roses out there . . .
(The cellular phone rings and Jim answers.)

JIM
(into phone)
Hello? Lola—yes . . . I don't know what happened . . . we were
disconnected . . . Oh no . . . I was about to say . . . I called
because I miss you and I'll pick you up at work and we can
walk home together . . . I love you . . . I love you . . . I—oh,
Lola—
(Exiting as Fred rants.)

FRED
I can actually make out some canals on Neptune—they could
be decoys—what did we do to make them so angry at us?
Nothing, you say? Think again . . . You're not the type for
an extramarital affair—and be thankful—the price is too
dear—love to Lola . . . Come in!

FADE OUT

OLD
SAYBROOK

*Curtain rises on a country home in Connecticut. A combination
of American antiques and contemporary furnishings—perhaps
a large stone fireplace—a staircase leading upstairs. Sheila and
Norman, who live there, are hosting a barbecue out in the back.
Sheila's sister, Jenny, and her husband, David, are the only
guests. Sound of geese honking.*

*Jenny, Sheila and Norman are fixing and/or refilling drinks
while they make small talk prior to going out back to cook.*

SHEILA
(looks out window and says wistfully)
Look, Norman, the geese are back.

NORMAN
Spoken like the tragic heroine of a Russian play.

JENNY
I hate Russian plays. Nothing happens and they charge the
same price as a musical.

SHEILA
To think that each year when the geese migrate south they pick
our little pond to lay over at for a few days.

NORMAN

I told you Old Saybrook is becoming the in place.

DAVID

What do the geese tell us about the inscrutable magnificence of nature?

SHEILA

What?

DAVID

That one day we all must grow old and decay. That's the message in all of nature.

JENNY

That's easy for him to say, he's a plastic surgeon and that message is on his business card.

SHEILA

Your wife got you, David.

DAVID
(toasts)
To the geese.

JENNY

Not the geese—to Norman and Sheila. Happy seventh anniversary.

NORMAN

Some of the happiest years of my life. Maybe two of them. Just joking.

SHEILA

Freud said there are no jokes.

NORMAN
(toasts)
To Sigmund Freud—the poet of penis envy.

DAVID
And now, if you'll all excuse me, I'm going into the den to
watch Tiger Woods—please don't disturb me until the steaks
come off the barbecue.
(Exits to den.)

JENNY
(exiting, to Sheila)
I'll make more ice—it's one of the only things I learned in
cooking school.

DAVID
(returning)
Where are the pistachio nuts?

SHEILA
I don't know . . .

DAVID
I can't watch golf without pistachio nuts.

SHEILA
David.

DAVID
They must be red—red, salted pistachio nuts.

SHEILA
(exiting to kitchen)
I have cashews—

DAVID
Cashews are basketball. Pistachios are golf.

NORMAN

David, just get out.

(David exits into den.)

I figured out what the geese symbolize. They symbolize impending disaster—the honking is a mating call and a mating call always spells trouble.

(Bell rings.)

NORMAN

(calls out)

Sheila, are you expecting anyone?

SHEILA

(returning to room)

No.

(They open the door and a comparable couple, Hal and Sandy Maxwell, stand there.)

Yes?

HAL

Hello—I hope we're not disturbing you.

SANDY

(a bit embarrassed)

This is silly, Hal.

HAL

I'm Hal Maxwell and this is my wife, Sandy. We were driving by and we don't want to intrude, but we used to live here.

SHEILA

Really?

SANDY

Yes—for nine years—we sold the place to a Mr. Krolian.

HAL

Max Krolian, a fairly well-known writer.

NORMAN

Sure—well, we've been here for about three years now.
Norman Pollack—Sheila's my wife. Please—come in.

SANDY

We don't want to bother you. We've moved to New Jersey and
we happened to be up here for one day antiquing and we were
so close.

SHEILA

Please—come in. Have a look around. Feel free.

NORMAN

So you used to live here?

SHEILA

Can we offer you a drink?

HAL

Oh God—I would love one.

SANDY

You have to drive.
(They have entered in deeper and look around.)

SHEILA

How does it look?

HAL

It brings back such memories.

NORMAN

What would you like?

HAL
What I would *like* is a single malt scotch but I will drink
anything.

NORMAN
And you?

SANDY
Oh, just a tiny bit of white wine if you have it.

NORMAN
We have no white but our martinis are colorless.
(Sandy laughs at Norman's joke.)

HAL
(at window)
Whose idea was it to put in a swimming pool?

NORMAN
We did that.

HAL
What shape is it?

NORMAN
Amoeba—an amoeba . . . it's an amoeba-shaped pool.

HAL
Those little germs . . .

SANDY
Hal—
(Jenny enters.)

SHEILA
Oh—Jenny—these are—

HAL
The Maxwells.

SHEILA
They used to live here.

SANDY
We just wanted to see the place again—we were married here.

JENNY
Oh—how sweet.

HAL
In that garden. Under a maple tree—now it's gone, there's a pool.

SHEILA
You hungry?

SANDY
No—

HAL
What are you telling them no, we're starved.

NORMAN
Well then, join us—we're barbecuing some steaks.

SANDY
No, we couldn't.

HAL
Er—medium rare.

DAVID
(emerges from den momentarily)
Who came in? I heard the bell ring just as Tiger was about to
putt. I think the noise made him miss.

JENNY
My husband—David, this is—

HAL
Hal and Sandy Maxwell—we used to live here.

DAVID
Oh really? Where did you put the pistachio nuts?

JENNY
David, they got married here.

DAVID
Oh great. Do you play golf?

HAL
No.

DAVID
Um, terrific. We must play sometime.

JENNY
In the winter it's the Knicks, in the summer it's golf—talk about Freud—he loves to watch young men put balls in holes. *(She goes.)*

HAL
Hey—what happened to the beautiful floor that was here?

NORMAN
Oh, er—we redid it.

HAL
Redid the random planking? Why?

NORMAN
We wanted something smoother.

SANDY
(with a look to her husband)
It's lovely—

HAL
This floor is the first spot we made love on—

SANDY
Hal—

HAL
—right here—where the coffee table is. It was smooth enough
for us.

SANDY
Hal—

SHEILA
Er—that's very romantic.

HAL
I think so. Sandy gets shy. It was a memorable moment.
Particularly since we were both married to different people
at the time.

SANDY
Hal!

SHEILA
Oh goodness.

HAL

Don't get the wrong impression. We were drunk, here alone,
there was an electrical storm, all the lights went out—suddenly
the room was illuminated by a flash of lightning and I saw
Sandy, her lips full, her hair wild from the intense humidity—
she beckoned me to her with the ever increasing promise of
sexual adventure.

SHEILA

What do you do, Mr. Maxwell?

HAL

Hal. I'm an accountant. See—her face fell.

SHEILA

What?

HAL

You figured me for a poet, right? I don't seem the type to be
crunching numbers for a business firm—do I?

SHEILA

I don't know—accountants can be poetic. You should see some
of our tax returns.

HAL

I feel there's more in me but I just don't have the courage.

SANDY

Hal would like to write the great American novel.

HAL

Play, Sandy, play—not novel. Although I have written a few
poems about the dangers of cholesterol. Sonnets.

SANDY

Did you know Mr. Krolian, the former owner?

NORMAN
Only by reputation.

HAL
I met him once when we sold the place. I tried to talk to him—
he was a difficult man to communicate with—but a very clever
writer.

NORMAN
Excuse me. I better go help her sister, Jenny—whenever she
tries to light the barbecue we wind up on the six o'clock news.
(He goes.)

SANDY
What does your husband do, Mrs.—

SHEILA
Sheila—he's a dentist.

HAL
Hey, that's almost as bad as me—ooh—well, I mean—er—what
does your sister do? Is she a model?

SHEILA
Jenny has a lingerie shop in Manhattan, and her husband
streamlines rear ends and I don't mean automotive work. He's
a plastic surgeon.
(Sandy laughs at Sheila's joke.)

SANDY
(looking out window)
The birdhouse is still up.

HAL
I designed and built that birdhouse myself.

SANDY
Based on the Guggenheim.

HAL
Hey—do you know about the secret vault?

SHEILA
No.

HAL
Yes, we wouldn't have known except we were told by the
original owner who built the house, Mr. Warner. He made
a hidden safe behind the fireplace.

SHEILA
No.

HAL
Yes—he did—

SANDY
Show her.

HAL
Here, it's right behind here, but you have to know where the
hidden latch is.
(Fiddling.)

SANDY
It's the top one and you pull the lever . . .

HAL
Here it—I got it—here you go . . .

SHEILA
(watches it open)
My God, you learn something new every day—

HAL
I can't believe you didn't know about it.

SHEILA
I had no idea! I lean on that mantel all the time—I never dreamed—a hidden safe—what's this?

SANDY
What is that?

SHEILA
(removes an old notebook—reads aloud)
I want to treasure these moments because they are the most passionate I've known.
(looks up)
Hmm. What is this?
(thumbs diary—reads)
Her quivering breasts under my hands caused us both to breathe heavy—

HAL
What'd you find there?

SHEILA
(reads)
Chronicle of my love affair with Sheila's sister, Jenny, by Norman Pollack—
(Sheila looks up.)

HAL
Norman Pollack—that's her husband.

SANDY
Well, it was nice meeting you . . .

SHEILA
Norman, can you come into the living room for a minute?

SANDY
We'll just let ourselves out . . .

NORMAN
(returning)
Did you say something, sweetheart?

SHEILA
You miserable duplicitous son of a bitch.

NORMAN
Pardon me?
(Realizes she's found something.)

SANDY
We love what you've done with the place—

SHEILA
This is yours.

NORMAN
What are you talking about?

HAL
She found your diary. You're in tremendous trouble.

NORMAN
My what? You must be kidding.

SHEILA
It's your name.

NORMAN
Oh Jesus, Sheila. There must be a hundred Norman Pollacks in
the phone book.

SHEILA
This is your handwriting.

NORMAN
Lots of people dot their i's with little circles.

SHEILA
There's a snapshot of you and Jenny with your hands on her breasts.

NORMAN
That's the only real piece of evidence you have.

SHEILA
(reads from diary)
I can no longer suppress the torrid feelings I have for Sheila's sister. Making love with Jenny is an ecstasy I have never experienced with anyone else.

SANDY
If you're ever in Nutley . . .

NORMAN
How did you find it?

HAL
When we bought the place I knew about the safe.

SANDY
Shut up, Hal.

NORMAN
You told her about it?

HAL
How did I know you were knocking off Jenny?

NORMAN

Now, Sheila, before you jump to any conclusions . . .

HAL

Norman, you don't get it—this is the smoking gun.

SANDY

Will you shut up, Hal?

SHEILA
(reads from diary)
I secretly slid my hand under her skirt as the four of us sat on the lawn at Tanglewood under the moonlight. For a moment I thought Sheila noticed—

HAL

Does it say what else happens?

NORMAN

Would you stay out of this!?

SHEILA

Today Jenny pretended she was a little girl and I slapped her rear end. She found it very erotic and we made love.

HAL

If I could just see the diary for a minute.

SANDY

Hal, butt out.

JENNY
(enters)
Norman—I accidentally let the fire go out in the barbecue.

SHEILA

Oh, "I accidentally let the fire go out in the barbecue"? Well, aren't you a bad little girl. Norman's going to have to give you another spanking.

JENNY

(doesn't get it)

What?

NORMAN

She found my diary.

JENNY

Your what?

SHEILA

(reading)

Today Jenny and I met at her place and made love in the same bed she shares with David.

JENNY

You keep a diary?

NORMAN

It was completely hidden. Till he told her where to find it.

HAL

How was I to know you were banging him? I innocently showed her the safe.

JENNY

Why in hell would you keep a diary?

HAL

They're very useful for tax purposes.

SANDY
Well—I'm sure you'll work things out—now, if you'll excuse—

SHEILA
Like hell—you stay right here—you're witnesses.

HAL
Witnesses? Is something gonna happen where you need witnesses?

SHEILA
How long have you two been cheating?

NORMAN
I'd hardly call a few rendezvous cheating.

SHEILA
(looking in diary)
According to this you had sexual relations four times on President's Day alone.

NORMAN
Well, yes, because Washington and Lincoln's birthdays are celebrated together.

HAL
I don't see what the big deal is here. Everybody in suburbia cheats.

SANDY
They do?

SHEILA
(reading diary)
Where did you learn those positions?

JENNY
Pilates.

HAL
(*laughing at her joke too hard*)
Did you hear that—

SANDY
I heard her, I heard her. We lived in suburbia—right here in
fact—I hope you didn't cheat, because I didn't.

HAL
Of course I wouldn't.

SANDY
Then why would you say something like that?

HAL
I was generalizing.

SANDY
Never with Holly?

HAL
Holly Fox? Gimme a break. Because she was an actress?

SANDY
Exactly—because you always insisted she wasn't so beautiful,
but on several occasions you said her name in your sleep.

HAL
You're projecting because you always had a little crush on her
brother.

SANDY
Believe me, if I wanted Ken Fox I would have had no problem.

HAL
Meaning what?

SANDY
Meaning he hit on me once a week for a year but I fended him off.

HAL
Well, this is the first I'm hearing about that.

SHEILA
How long have you two been having this tempestuous affair?

NORMAN
(simultaneously with Jenny)
Not long.

JENNY
Three years.

NORMAN
Six months.

JENNY
A year.

NORMAN
And a half.

JENNY
Not long.

NORMAN
There was a lot of downtime.

SHEILA
How could you do it, you're my sister!

JENNY
What can I say, we fell in love.

NORMAN
It wasn't love, it was pure sex.

JENNY
You said it was love.

NORMAN
I never actually used that word—I said I "care" for you—
I "miss" you—I "need" you—I "can't live without you"
—but not love.

SHEILA
All this time you've been sharing my bed you've been sleeping
with Jenny.

NORMAN
Can I help it if she seduced me?

JENNY
I seduced you?

NORMAN
Three years ago I walked into her lingerie shop—to buy you
a present—I found something that looked nice—I asked if it
would fit you—she said she was about your size, she'd try it
on—I could see it—we both went into the changing booth—
she slipped into it—

HAL
Into what?

NORMAN
A thong—she was wearing a thong.

SANDY
(to Hal)
Will you butt out.

HAL
I'm trying to follow the narrative.

SANDY
You find her attractive, don't you?

SHEILA
You too?

HAL
What?

SANDY
I heard you ask Sheila if her sister was a model—and you've
been champing at the bit to get your hands on that diary.

HAL
Can I help it if I'm an inadvertent participant in this all-too-
human drama?

SHEILA
(handing him diary)
Here—you appreciate literature—

HAL
I really don't—
(Has accepted diary and becomes riveted by it.)

SANDY
Oh go ahead, Hal, take it. I'm sure you'll find the details of her
sexual activities gratifying.

HAL
(leafing through book)
Well, maybe to—uh—uh—

SANDY
Let's say to a live male under ninety.

HAL
Gee, Sandy, I only wish you were half as adventurous as she is.

SANDY
Over my dead body.

HAL
I'm not discussing our sex life.

SANDY
I'm sorry if I disappoint you.

HAL
Look, we've been through it . . . I'm only saying, if you were
willing to experiment once in a while . . .

SANDY
If by experimenting you mean a threesome with Holly Fox.

HAL
Well, what is your idea of an experiment?

SANDY
I don't think about experimenting. We're making love, not
working on a science grant.

SHEILA
You always read about those perverted dentists who have sex
with their unconscious patients during root canal.

NORMAN

I'm not a perverted dentist. I'm a perverted orthodontist—you never got that straight. Look, I take full responsibility. If you have to blame someone, blame me.

SHEILA

Who the hell do you think I'm blaming?

DAVID

(emerges from den)

Tiger Woods just bogeyed a hole.

HAL

So did Norman.

DAVID

It's very exciting.

SHEILA

Join us, David, we have something to show you.

DAVID

Can't it wait?

SHEILA

I don't know, it's very hot.

JENNY

Stop being so vicious.

SHEILA

Come sit with me for a moment, David.

HAL

Quick, Sandy—do you have our camcorder?

SANDY
It's in the car.

SHEILA
Read this diary, David—see if you recognize any of the
protagonists.

DAVID
(taking diary)
What is this? Tiger Woods is going to set a record.

NORMAN
Let the man enjoy his golf. This doesn't concern him.

HAL
Oh, Norman—he's bound to have some marginal interest.
(David reads.)

SHEILA
What do you think, David—recognize the lead characters?

HAL
Of course he does.

DAVID
The people?

SHEILA
Yes, the married woman called Jenny and the dentist.

DAVID
The married woman, Jenny? Where would I recognize her
from?

SHEILA
Try breakfast.

DAVID

What is this, some silly piece of porn? Why should I read it, I'm watching the U.S. Open.

SHEILA

You're married to the U.S. Open.

NORMAN

Jenny—

SHEILA

Norman!

NORMAN

Sheila.

DAVID

What? What am I missing?

HAL

Can I give him a hint?

SANDY

Will you keep out.

HAL

I can't believe he can't get it.

SHEILA

You find it a coincidence the man's name is Norman and the woman's is Jenny?

DAVID

No—why?

SHEILA

Your wife's name is Jenny, my husband's name is Norman.

DAVID
So?

SANDY
This guy's a doctor?

SHEILA
You recognize the two people in this photo?

NORMAN
Sheila—

HAL
I've heard of denial—

DAVID
Yes—that's your husband with some woman.

SHEILA
Uh-huh—you see Norman's tongue?

DAVID
Yes.

SHEILA
Where is it?

DAVID
In his mouth.

SHEILA
The other end.

DAVID
In this woman's ear.

SHEILA
And his hands?

DAVID
(studies photo)
Hmmm—Norman, is this some new dental procedure?

SHEILA
And you don't recognize the woman?

DAVID
She's definitely familiar.

SHEILA
Shall I give you a clue?

JENNY
I can't stand this.

SHEILA
Remember how years ago you met a young woman at a dinner party and you hit it off and began dating?

DAVID
Yes—and we both loved Tolstoy and French films and sailing—and I married her—Jenny—so what is your point? That the woman in the diary—in the photo—resembles Jenny? That the woman resembles Jenny? That the woman resembles Jenny? That the woman resembles Jenny? That the woman—that the woman's Jenny—it's Jenny—I got it—I got it.

HAL
I'd never let this guy do my plastic surgery.

JENNY
You're so cruel, Sheila.

DAVID
(stunned)
This *is* you—you're her—she's you—she's who you are—

JENNY
David, try and understand—apart from the sex it was platonic.

HAL
What is the problem here? If she can discuss Tolstoy and
foreign films and also does all this you've hit the jackpot.

SANDY
You have a thing for her—I felt that right off.

HAL
All I'm saying is that in addition to a cultivated wife and good
mother it's nice if you go to bed each night with a real freak.

SANDY
I don't believe I'm hearing this.

DAVID
I'm stunned—I'm stupefied. I didn't even know—who is the
guy again?

SHEILA
Norman—Norman—right here.

NORMAN
Oh stop it, Sheila. I've been having an affair with Jenny.

DAVID
Jenny—a woman with the same name as my wife?

SHEILA
The trauma's too much.

DAVID

A love affair?

HAL

This guy kills me—what other kind of affair is there?

DAVID

But that means Norman and Jenny are sleeping with each other.

JENNY

Yes, David, we slept together—but if it's any consolation, there was very little foreplay.

SHEILA

That sounds like Norman.

DAVID

But he's my brother-in-law and she's my wife. And who are the people in the picture?

SHEILA

He's lost it.

DAVID

Excuse me.
(Exits.)

HAL

If he's going to see Tiger Woods now, that's what I call a sports fan.

SHEILA

Of course this means a divorce.

JENNY

Sheila, I may have cheated physically, but mentally I've been a loyal sibling.

SHEILA

Sibling? How dare you? You're no longer my sister. From this moment on, the most you could ever be to me is a niece.

NORMAN

Sheila, Sheila . . . how can I make this up to you?

SHEILA

The firm of Rifkin and Abramowitz will let you know.

DAVID

(enters with rifle)

And now—prepare to die.

JENNY

David!

NORMAN

All right, let's not play games. That's a loaded shotgun.

DAVID

Back off, Norman! Back off! Everybody in this room is going to die and then I'm putting the barrel in my mouth and squeezing the trigger.

HAL

(looks at watch)

Oh, is it six already? We have tickets to *Mamma Mia!*

DAVID

Not so fast, I said everybody.

HAL

We just drove up to see the house.

JENNY

David, you have that look in your eye.

DAVID

First you and Norman, then Sheila.

SHEILA

Why me? What the hell did I do? I got cheated on like you.

DAVID

You found the diary.

SHEILA

He showed me where.

DAVID

Believe me, he's going too.

SANDY

We're innocent bystanders.

DAVID

That makes the news story perfect, doesn't it? The adulterous couple, the poor husband and wife—two perfectly innocent bystanders.

HAL

You're crazy.

DAVID

That's what they said about the Son of Sam.

HAL

Yes—so—they were right.

JENNY

He's flipped out.

HAL

But you can't kill *us*—we didn't do anything. I never cheated. I could have—and believe me, I wanted to.

SANDY

You did?

HAL

Well, face it, Sandy, you can be a cold fish.

SANDY

Me?

HAL

That's right—she is the opposite of Jenny—will not ever try anything new.

SANDY

Well, maybe if you'd romance me once in a while instead of doing everything so fast.

HAL

I'm only trying to get it done before the headache sets in.

DAVID

Shut up! Who let them in?! It's unfortunate you wandered in, but that's life—full of ironies—some of them pleasant, some rather ugly—I've never thought life was a gift—it's a burden—a sentence—cruel and unusual punishment—everybody say your prayers—
(They huddle together as he cocks his shotgun. Suddenly they hear a noise and a man comes down the stairs. The man is tied up and gagged, apparently having gotten loose from a chair. His arms are still tied and he makes muffled, gagged sounds.)

DAVID
(noticing him)
Oh no—

SHEILA
Oh Christ.

NORMAN
I thought—

SHEILA
Oh brother.

JENNY
Help! Help!
(Hal and Sandy—one or both run to the man and take off his gag.)

DAVID
Don't do that—don't—oh—

MAX
OK—the party's over.

SANDY
Who are you?

JENNY
Who tied him up?

DAVID
It was Norman.

SHEILA
This sinks us.

HAL

Aren't you Mr. Krolian? I'm Hal Maxwell. I sold you this
house a few years ago. Sandy, it's Max Krolian—

MAX
(referring to ropes)
Get these off me.

HAL
(untying him)
What's going on?

MAX

These wild animals—I created them—then they turned on me.

DAVID

Ah, you're incompetent.

MAX

They're from my pen.

SANDY
What is this?

JENNY
The game's up—why don't you tell 'em the truth?

HAL
What?

NORMAN
He had an idea for a play—which he was writing—

SHEILA
He invented us.

DAVID
From his fertile imagination.

SHEILA
He wrote half the play.

MAX
That's right—and I couldn't figure out where I was going with it—it wasn't coming—

DAVID
He was blocked.

MAX
Sometimes an idea seems great, but after you work on it for a while it just doesn't go anyplace.

SHEILA
But by then it was too late. We were born.

DAVID
Invented.

MAX
Created. I had half a play.

HAL
You always had a flair for creating wonderful live characters with fascinating problems and great dialogue.

NORMAN
So then what does he do?

JENNY
He gave up the idea.

NORMAN

He threw the half-finished play in the drawer.

DAVID

It's dark in the drawer.

MAX

What else could I do? I had no finish.

DAVID

I hated the goddamned drawer.

SHEILA

I mean, picture you and your wife in a drawer.

JENNY

There's nothing to do in a drawer.

NORMAN

It sucks.

SHEILA

Then Jenny got the idea that we push it open and escape into the world.

MAX

I thought I heard the drawer opening—by the time I turned around they were all over me.

SANDY

What did you think you'd do once you broke out?

SHEILA

We hoped we could figure out some way to finish his third act.

NORMAN

So we could have a life every night in theatres—forever.

JENNY

What's the alternative? To be half-finished in a dark drawer?

DAVID

I'm not going back in the drawer! I'm not going back in the
drawer! I'm not going—
(Norman slaps David.)

MAX

I've thought and thought—I can't figure where it goes.

HAL

Well, let's analyze what we've got . . . she discovers her sister is
having an affair with her husband.

MAX

Who are you?

HAL

Hal Maxwell—I sold you—

MAX

The accountant?

HAL

I've always wanted to write a play.

MAX

So does everyone.

HAL

Why are they having an affair? What's wrong with their
marriage?

NORMAN

I'm bored with Sheila.

SHEILA
Why?

NORMAN
I don't know.

MAX
Don't ask me. I'm written out.

HAL
Why does any husband get bored with his wife? Because with
time they get too familiar. The excitement wanes—they're
always together around the house—they see each other
undressed—there's no more mystery—now even his
secretary is sexier to him—or the next-door neighbor.

JENNY
That's not realistic.

HAL
How would you know? You're not even well written. It's very
realistic—it happens all the time. Take it from me.

SANDY
It does?

HAL
I mean, freshness in marriage has to be worked on—otherwise,
there's no music in a relationship, and music is everything.

SANDY
What if the husband was once romantic but he gradually takes
the wife for granted? What used to be a relationship full of
imaginative, charming surprises is now just a life together by
the numbers, with them having sex but not making love.

HAL

I'd hardly find that a believable conflict.

SANDY

I think many women would identify with it.

HAL

Too far-out.

SHEILA

I think it sounds very plausible.

JENNY

Very close to the bone.

SANDY

Very.

DAVID

And you think it can just evaporate? Even if at one time they loved one another?

MAX

That's one of the sad truths of existence. Nothing in this world is permanent. Even the characters created by the great Shakespeare will, in millions of years, cease to exist—when the universe runs its course and the lights go out.

DAVID

Jesus, I think I'll just go back and watch Tiger Woods. The hell with it all.

NORMAN

That's right. What's it all mean if the cosmos breaks apart and everything finally vanishes?

JENNY

That's why it's important to be held and squeezed now—by anyone willing to do the squeezing.

SHEILA

Don't try to justify screwing my husband on existential grounds.

HAL

What if you and David were also having an affair?

MAX

I thought of that, but then it starts to become silly.

JENNY

But if life is anything, it's silly.

DAVID

That's right. The philosophers call it absurd, but what they really mean is silly.

MAX

The problem is, it implies everyone is unfaithful, but it's not accurate.

HAL

But it doesn't have to be accurate if it's funny. Art is different from life.

MAX

Art is the mirror of life.

HAL

Speaking of mirrors, I always wanted to put a mirror on the ceiling over our bed, but she wouldn't go for it.

SANDY
It's the dumbest thing I ever heard.

HAL
It's sexy.

SANDY
It's adolescent. I want to make love, not watch two images of
each other having intercourse—from that perspective I'll just
see your behind going up and down.

HAL
Why do you always ridicule my needs? Then you wonder why
I sit and daydream about Holly Fox.

SANDY
Just don't tell her your mirror idea, she'll burst out laughing.

HAL
If you must know, we've done it in front of a mirror.

SANDY
In your fantasies.

HAL
In your bathroom.

SANDY
What?

DAVID
Aha! This is a juicier story than ours.

HAL
Not that I loved her or that we had an affair or anything. It was
a one-shot deal.

SANDY
You and Holly Fox?

HAL
What are you acting so surprised? You've accused me of it
jokingly for two years.

SANDY
I was joking.

HAL
There are no jokes. Freud said that.

SHEILA
That's my line.

SANDY
Besides, you always swore she didn't appeal to you.

HAL
That's right, I swore—I held up my right hand—I'm an
agnostic.

NORMAN
Be reasonable, Sandy. No husband admits to having slept with
another woman.

SANDY
He just did.

MAX
That's why my wife left me. That's why I bought your house to
live alone and keep out of the rat race of romantic relationships.
I was having an affair with my wife's mother.

NORMAN
My God—why isn't that in our story—it's great.

MAX

Because no one would believe it. Her father was a well-known
film star—well, I don't have to tell you—he divorced her
biological mother and married their au pair girl—so my
wife now had a mother ten years younger than she.

JENNY

A stepmother.

MAX

It's semantics—meanwhile I was boffing her.

DAVID

So you're also cheating on your father-in-law.

MAX

That's OK because he was a shoe fetishist who could only get
aroused if Prada was having a sale.

SHEILA

This does strain credulity.

MAX

My wife's mother kept a diary. Very graphic. Our intimacies—
our lovemaking. Details. Names. She thought it romantic.
One night my wife said to her, I'm going to the Hamptons
tomorrow—I need a good book for the beach. Thinking it was
her leather-bound volume of Henry James, she mistakenly gave
her the leather-bound diary. I was with my wife when she read
it on the beach. A change came over her—a physical change—
like when the full moon comes out in a Wolfman movie.

HAL

So that's where you got the idea.

NORMAN

What'd you do?

MAX

What could I do? I denied it.

NORMAN

What'd she do?

MAX

She tried to drown herself. She ran into the ocean but only succeeded in getting stung by a jellyfish. It made her lips swell up. Suddenly with those big lips she looked sexy, and I fell back in love with her. Of course, when the swelling went down she got on my nerves again.

HAL

Well, I *wasn't* having an affair—mine was a onetime thing. At our New Year's Eve party. Everyone was downstairs drinking, partying—I happened to walk past your bathroom upstairs, Holly was in it and asked if we had any Q-tips, so I went in to help her find them, closed the door and did it with her.

DAVID

Why did she need Q-tips?

JENNY

What's the difference!?

NORMAN

Who cares about the goddamn Q-tips?

SANDY

They'd been making eyes at each other for months.

HAL

That's pure projection. You were the one with big eyes for her brother.

SANDY

If you were more perceptive you would have known I had no
interest in Ken Fox.

HAL

No?

SANDY

No. If I ever would have strayed at all it would have been with
Howard Nadleman.

HAL

Nadleman? The real estate agent?

SANDY

Howard Nadleman knows how to make a woman feel her
sexuality.

HAL

What does that mean?

SANDY

Nothing.

HAL

You had a one-night stand with Howard Nadleman?

SANDY

No.

HAL

Thank God for that.

SANDY

We had a long romance.

HAL
You had a romance with Howard Nadleman?

SANDY
Yes, I did.

HAL
Don't deny it.

SANDY
As long as we're coming clean, I may as well be honest too.

HAL
A minute ago you said, "if I ever would have strayed at all," implying you never strayed.

SANDY
I can't live this lie anymore. With all due respect to you, I've been sleeping with Howard Nadleman.

DAVID
Go, Nadleman!

HAL
Don't make me laugh.

SANDY
I've always loved you, Hal—you know that. But what does a person do when the romance fades—when the passion drains away and you still love and respect your spouse—you cheat on him.

NORMAN
That's what I was trying to explain to Sheila.

HAL
How many times did you sleep with Howard?

SANDY

Do numbers ever really tell you anything?

HAL

Yes, I'm an accountant.

SANDY

Let's put it this way—I don't go for psychoanalysis.

HAL

You mean—all those Wednesdays, Thursdays and Saturdays—

SANDY

There is no Doctor Fineglass.

HAL

And I thought your depression was lifting.

SANDY

It was.

HAL

But a hundred and sixty dollars an hour?

SANDY

That was for the hotel rooms.

HAL

I was paying for your hotel rooms three days a week with
Howard Nadleman all year?

SANDY

Didn't you notice it was strange I had the only shrink who
didn't take August off?

DAVID
It turns out their life is the farce, not ours.

SHEILA
The farce, or is it tragedy?

NORMAN
Why is it tragedy?

SHEILA
It's a sorry situation—two people who must've loved one another at one time—obviously still do—but the initial excitement drains from their marriage . . .

JENNY
But no one can sustain that first rush of excitement.

DAVID
That's right—we settle in—the sexual passion is replaced by other things—shared experiences—children—beastiality.

HAL
Is it still going on with you and Nadleman?

SANDY
No—remember some months ago he suffered a brain concussion?

HAL
Yes—he's never been the same—how did it happen?

SANDY
The mirror on the ceiling over the bed fell on him.

HAL
Oh God! Him and not me!

DAVID

I'll tell you why their situation is farce—because they're pathetic. They lack tragic stature. What is he, an accountant? And she's a housewife. This is not *Hamlet* or *Medea*.

HAL

Oh please—you don't have to be a prince to suffer—there's millions of people out there every bit as tortured as Hamlet. They're Hamlet on Prozac.

SANDY

And jealous as Medea.

MAX

Therefore, what can I conclude? Everybody has their dark secrets, their longings, their lusts, their awful needs—so if life is to continue one must choose to forgive.

NORMAN

And that's where our play should go. So I took a momentary fancy to your sister—big deal—so maybe you should write it so that Sheila and David once spent a passionate night together—so we all learn each other's pathetic shortcomings and we forgive each other.

JENNY

Yes. And the audience laughs at all of us and they escape from their own sad lives for a brief moment and then we kiss and make up.

MAX

Forgiveness—it gives this little sex farce dimension and heart.

SHEILA

That's right. Who am I to judge others and throw away years of closeness and love because my husband the dentist was drilling my sister?

JENNY

We'll change—we'll make amends. Where there's life there's hope.

SANDY

But how is forgiveness different than just sweeping all your problems under the rug?

MAX

It's much grander—it takes a bigger person—forgiveness is divine.

JENNY

And maybe it's the same but it sounds better.

MAX

I like it—it's funny, it's sad, and best of all, it's commercial. Come—let's go to my study so I can complete the third act while it's all fresh—I feel my writer's block lifting. The key word is "commercial"—I'm sorry, "forgiveness"—the key word is "forgiveness."
(They go upstairs together. The Maxwells look at each other.)

HAL

I don't think I can forgive you, Sandy.

SANDY

No. Nor I, you.

HAL

I don't know why. I know Max Krolian is right—he's a deep playwright.

SANDY

It's easy to forgive in fiction—the author can manipulate reality. And as you say, Krolian's a clever craftsman.

HAL

I can't believe you had a long affair with Howard Nadleman—
he was probably getting even with me for the audit.

SANDY

It had nothing to do with you—everything is not always about
you.

HAL

Was I such an unromantic husband?

SANDY

As the years went by you stopped trying.

HAL

I became discouraged. You started taking me for granted too.

SANDY

All those imaginary characters can be rewritten—their lives
erased, begun again—but we've said and done things that can
never be erased.

HAL

The tragic part is that I love you.

SANDY

And I love you, but it's pathetic, not tragic.

HAL

If I took that rifle and killed us both I could redeem our
infidelities with one grand gesture.

SANDY

You're not the type, Hal. Accountants don't commit suicide and
find redemption—they usually just vanish and turn up in the
Cayman Islands.

HAL
What do you want to do?

SANDY
What can we do? Sweep the painful aspects of the relationship under the rug and call it forgiveness or get a divorce.

HAL
Sandy—this was the first room we made love in. Can't we start over?

SANDY
Clean starts work better in fiction.

HAL
But every life needs a little fiction in it—too much reality is a very nasty thing.

SANDY
Maybe now that everything's out in the open . . . What's that honking sound?

HAL
(to window)
Look at all those geese.

SANDY
(joining him)
My goodness—we never had geese when we lived here.

HAL
It's a symbol.

SANDY
Of what?

HAL

Of a fresh start—of geese where geese never were. Today was a
day full of symbols—full of writing, of characters, of literature.
The poet that beats 'neath the breast of this accountant came
out and I helped Max Krolian write a warm ending to his play—
only you and I remained unresolved, undecided and confused
—we were looking for some sign—some way to recapture the
music in our relationship and then—the honking of the geese—

SANDY

And you see it as a symbol.

HAL

Don't you see, Sandy? Can't you see what they're trying to tell
us? Don't you know one simple fact about geese? Geese mate
forever.

SANDY

Do geese have affairs?

HAL

If they do they work it out somehow—it's all in nature's
design.

SANDY

Could it really be my husband is a poet trapped in the body of
a CPA?
(Sound of geese honking, and music rises.)
Kiss.

FADE OUT

CENTRAL
PARK
WEST

The Central Park West apartment of Phyllis and Sam Riggs.
It is spacious with dark woods and books. They live there, and it
also is where Phyllis practices her psychoanalysis. The layout
enables a patient to enter the front door and privately wait,
then privately go into the inner sanctum for his or her session.
What we see predominantly is the large living room and the
front door, a set of doors leading to other rooms.

It is about 6:00 P.M. on a November Saturday. No one is
onstage as we hear ringing at the door and, since it receives
no response, knocking. The knocking continues through the
following dialogue.

CAROL
(offstage)
Phyllis? Phyllis?
(Phyllis enters from SR fully dressed. She sits on the SR end of
the sofa.)
Phyllis! It's Carol.

PHYLLIS
I'm coming.

CAROL
Are you OK?

PHYLLIS
I'm soaking wet. You caught me in the shower.
(Phyllis crosses US to bar. Pours a drink. Downs it. More door buzzing and knocking from Carol.)
All right. I'm dressed.
(Phyllis crosses US to front door and opens it to let Carol in.)

CAROL
Are you all right?

PHYLLIS
No details, please.

CAROL
No details of what?

PHYLLIS
I *said* let's not get into it.

CAROL
Is everyone OK?

PHYLLIS
Everyone? You mean in the third-world countries too?

CAROL
The third-world countries?

PHYLLIS
You mean like Zimbabwe?

CAROL
Did something happen in Africa?

PHYLLIS

My God—you're so literal—it's such a curse to be literal. A waste of wit—all my jokes and little ironies go straight down the toilet.

CAROL

What's going on?

PHYLLIS

The reference to third-world countries is a one-liner meant to lighten imperceptibly the pain of this all-too-human tragedy we are faced with.

CAROL

What tragedy?

PHYLLIS

Please—I would hardly call this a tragedy.

CAROL

How long have you been drinking?

PHYLLIS

Long enough to achieve a state of one with nature—or put another way—a drunken stupor. What's the difference between sushi and pussy?

CAROL

Phyllis—

PHYLLIS

Rice. One of my patients told it to me. Don't try and deconstruct it, Carol—it's a phenomenon too abstract for your thought process—it's called humor.

CAROL
I'll make some coffee.

PHYLLIS
Only if *you* want it. I'm content to stay with my special hyper-dry martini—all gin and I lightly say the word "vermouth."

CAROL
What happened?

PHYLLIS
What are you accusing me of?

CAROL
What is the emergency?

PHYLLIS
What emergency?

CAROL
The message on my service.

PHYLLIS
(noticing her garment)
Where'd you get that?

CAROL
That what?

PHYLLIS
Not them there eyes, honey—the coat.

CAROL
This coat?

PHYLLIS
Now you got it.

CAROL
You've seen this coat a hundred times.

PHYLLIS
I have?

CAROL
Including yesterday.

PHYLLIS
One of my patients was wearing this fur coat—OK? Made up
of many skins.

CAROL
What's the emergency?

PHYLLIS
And these acned fanatics accosted her right on Fifth Avenue.
Those ones who would bomb all furriers—and they started
harassing her and then some of the antivivisectionists or
whatever they are got physical and they pulled her coat off
and underneath she was stark naked.

CAROL
Why?

PHYLLIS
Because she's a whore. She's a high-priced whore and I've been
treating her for research on my book and she was on an out-
call to a guy who wanted a woman to knock on his door in a fur
coat and nothing under it. So there she was on Fifth Avenue
and Fifty-seventh Street with her fur coat on the pavement
and her body exposed for all New York to enjoy—a medley of
beavers. Now, where were we?

CAROL
Is Sam all right?

PHYLLIS
No details, please.

CAROL
Is he?

PHYLLIS
He's fine. The worst threat to Sam's health in his fifty years has
been one case of chapped lips.

CAROL
And the boys?

PHYLLIS
Away—away down south in the land of cotton—

CAROL
And there's no problem with them at school?

PHYLLIS
They don't cotton to it—and the university doesn't cotton to
them. God, there's so much cotton here my mouth is dry.
(She pours a drink.)

CAROL
Why are you so distraught?

PHYLLIS
Distraught? I haven't even reacted yet—this is nothing—you
got that? Nothing—nada—zilch—where'd you get that coat?

CAROL
Bloomingdale's. Last year.

PHYLLIS
And you wear it a lot?

CAROL
All the time.

PHYLLIS
What animal?

CAROL
It's a good old Republican cloth coat. Now, why did you leave
that hysterical message?

PHYLLIS
I'd rather not discuss it.

CAROL
You'd rather not discuss it? I get this frantic, desperate
message—emergency, crisis—help. I called you ten times.

PHYLLIS
Was that you?

CAROL
It sure was.

PHYLLIS
Usually I can tell your ring. It's tremulous and tentative.

CAROL
Where's Sam? What's wrong?

PHYLLIS
I don't want to tell you.

CAROL
Why'd you call me?

PHYLLIS
Because I have to talk to someone.

CAROL
So talk.

PHYLLIS
Can we not discuss it?

CAROL
Phyllis—

PHYLLIS
Can't you see I'm being evasive?

CAROL
Why?

PHYLLIS
I'm sorry if I inconvenienced you.

CAROL
You didn't.

PHYLLIS
Did you and Howard have plans?

CAROL
No. I was at Sotheby's.

PHYLLIS
What'd you get?

CAROL
Nothing. They're auctioning off baseball cards and Howard wanted to see them and it's the last day.

PHYLLIS
So you two did have plans.

CAROL

No, because Howard couldn't go because today is the day he had to drive his father to Westchester and put him in the home.

PHYLLIS

How sad.

CAROL

He's ninety-three—he had a good life—or maybe it was a lousy life—but a long one. And he never had any health problems or so they thought, except what they didn't know was that he was having a long series of silent strokes and soon he started forgetting things, then hearing musical sounds, and finally he tried to reenlist in the army.

PHYLLIS

Howard must be devastated.

CAROL
(looking at her watch)
I left a message for him to meet me here. So what's going on?

PHYLLIS

Look how she probes.

CAROL

Stop it. You called me.

PHYLLIS

But you always probe—you're always fishing for information.

CAROL

How am I fishing? You call and say it's life and death. I—

PHYLLIS
(softly)
I'm ashamed to tell you what happened, Carol.

CAROL
(realizing for the first time the broken statuette)
Hey—your fertility statue is broken—the penis came off.

PHYLLIS
That's OK—I'll just bring it to my penis repairman.

CAROL
In fact, the place looks a little in disarray.

PHYLLIS
Aren't you observant.

CAROL
What'd you do, get robbed?

PHYLLIS
On the other hand, I did fail to notice that drop-dead cloth coat
from Bloomingdale's after repeated exposure to it. What color
is that coat? Puce?

CAROL
It's yellowish.

PHYLLIS
It's puce.

CAROL
OK, it's puce.

PHYLLIS
You should never wear puce. It doesn't go with hazel eyes.

CAROL
I don't have hazel eyes.

PHYLLIS
One of them is—the one that looks off that way—

CAROL
Stop being evil, Phyllis. Did you have a fight with Sam?

PHYLLIS
Not exactly—

CAROL
Meaning? God, this is like pulling teeth.

PHYLLIS
Your teeth are good. The caps were worth every penny.

CAROL
(dryly)
Thank you.

PHYLLIS
Now, the chin tuck on the other hand . . .

CAROL
You didn't have a fight with Sam?

PHYLLIS
Yes, I did—

CAROL
You said, not exactly—

PHYLLIS
Not exactly what?

CAROL
Not exactly a fight—I said, did you and Sam have a fight and
you said—

PHYLLIS
I did, Sam did not.

CAROL
What did Sam do while you were fighting?

PHYLLIS
He watched me fight.

CAROL
And then?

PHYLLIS
And then he ducked—

CAROL
You hit him?

PHYLLIS
I missed him—I threw this statue at him in a desperate attempt to become a widow.

CAROL
My God—

PHYLLIS
Would you like another drink?

CAROL
What happened?

PHYLLIS
Oh, Carol—Carol—Carol—Carol—friend Carol.

CAROL
I think I am going to need that drink.

PHYLLIS
He left me.

CAROL
He did?

PHYLLIS
Yes.

CAROL
How do you know?

PHYLLIS
How do I know? How do I know he left me? Because he walked
out the door with his belongings and he's getting a divorce.

CAROL
I have to sit down—my legs are weak.

PHYLLIS
Your legs are weak?

CAROL
What reason did he give?

PHYLLIS
He doesn't love me—he doesn't like to be around me—it gives
him the dry heaves to imagine himself going through the
joyless choreography of sex with me anymore. Those are the
vague reasons he gives, but I think he's just being polite. I think
he really doesn't like my cooking.

CAROL
Out of left field.

PHYLLIS

Well, to me it was out of left field but I'm not perceptive—I'm just an analyst.

CAROL

He never said anything—or hinted?

PHYLLIS

He never said anything—but that was probably because we never spoke.

CAROL

Well, Phyllis—

PHYLLIS

I mean, we spoke—it wasn't just "pass the salt," although that came up once in a while too.

CAROL

You must have had conversations where he indicated something—

PHYLLIS

Let me put it to you this way—we both spoke but at the same time. What I mean is, there were two speakers but no listeners.

CAROL

Failure to communicate.

PHYLLIS

God, Carol, how you cut right to the heart of things.

CAROL

Well, it should have told you something.

PHYLLIS

It did.

CAROL
Well, what?

PHYLLIS
I don't know, I wasn't listening, I was talking.

CAROL
And the sex began to fall off.

PHYLLIS
How did you know?

CAROL
I didn't, I'm assuming.

PHYLLIS
Well, don't assume. People can stop communicating verbally and the sex can still be ferocious.

CAROL
OK—so the sex was great.

PHYLLIS
Great? It was better than great—it gave him the dry heaves.

CAROL
Somewhere along the line the lovemaking slips away—but that's only because something deeper has already slipped away. Or is it the other way around? The sex goes and then everything else loses all its luster. The point is—everything is ephemeral.

PHYLLIS
Is it, Carol?

CAROL
Oh—I don't know—you're asking the wrong person.

PHYLLIS
I don't remember asking.

CAROL
So he didn't say anything other than he was leaving?

PHYLLIS
Like what?

CAROL
Anything?

PHYLLIS
Yeah, he said even though it wasn't part of our prenuptial agreement, he'd go on paying for my delivery of the Sunday *Times.*

CAROL
But he didn't say where he was going?

PHYLLIS
(something setting in)
I'm beginning to react to it now.

CAROL
Phyllis, you've been reacting—

PHYLLIS
No—reacting would be if I took all these important papers—all his work which he still needs and did this to them.
(tears them up)
That would be a reaction, but I'm not a spiteful person—I'm not vengeful, I'm generous and mature.

CAROL
Take it easy!
(Phyllis crosses to Sam's briefcase on coffee table. She dumps out the contents and throws the briefcase across the stage.)

PHYLLIS
(as she tears up strewn documents)
We were just talking about redoing the house in Amagansett.
I said, we haven't touched it since we first bought it—I said, let's get Paul and Cindi's architect and redo it all—he said, Phyllis, I want to talk to you—I said, the house is so well situated on the bay and we've had such good times there—he said, Phyllis, I don't know how to tell you this but I want out—I didn't hear him—it was one of those conversations where nobody listens—I said, we always wanted picture windows and a bigger bathroom—he said, Phyllis, I'm leaving you—and I said, with one of those showers with many spigots that spray you from all sides—and he grabbed me and said, Phyllis, I don't love you anymore—I want a new life—I want out, I want out, *I want out*! And I said, what color should we paint the guest room?

CAROL
What did he say?

PHYLLIS
He didn't say anything, he began shaking me around the neck and after about three minutes of shaking I began to realize he was trying to tell me something.

CAROL
Exactly what did he tell you?

PHYLLIS
He said, I'm in love with another woman.
(Carol coughs and nearly gags on her drink.)

PHYLLIS

Are you OK? Or do I have to do the Heimlich maneuver?

CAROL

Did he say who she was?

PHYLLIS

I have a patient who gagged on a fish bone at Le Bernardin and a stranger came up behind her and performed the Heimlich maneuver on her and it aroused her—and now wherever she dines, she gags—

CAROL

Did he say who he was leaving you for?

PHYLLIS

Why do you look so uncomfortable?

CAROL

I'm not—although I am beginning to feel this drink.

PHYLLIS

At first I thought it was Anne Dreyfuss.

CAROL

Anne Dreyfuss? The decorator?

PHYLLIS

She likes all the stuff he likes—boating, the woods, skiing—

CAROL

He'd never take up with Anne Dreyfuss.

PHYLLIS

How do *you* know?

CAROL

What do you mean, how do I know? I know Sam too.

PHYLLIS

Not as well as me.

CAROL

I didn't say that. I mean, we're all friends for years.

PHYLLIS

How many years?

CAROL

Five—almost six—what has that got to do with anything?
I can't see Sam with Anne Dreyfuss. She's a whiner—with
a very annoying personality and if I may say so, no fanny.

PHYLLIS

I thought also it might be Nonny—the girl in his law firm.
She's a partner now . . .

CAROL

I don't know Nonny—what's she like?

PHYLLIS

Buxom and cute. With an erotic overbite. It's not Nonny.

CAROL

The point is you obviously don't know who he's gone off with.

PHYLLIS

The point is I do. Or at least I think I figured it out.

CAROL

You know, I really don't feel well.

PHYLLIS
Gee you're pale—either pale or puce.

CAROL
I can't drink. I feel queasy.

PHYLLIS
You're probably motion sick—from squirming.

CAROL
I'm nauseated.

PHYLLIS
Nauseating?

CAROL
Nauseated.

PHYLLIS
(crosses out to get Compazine)
I may have some Compazine suppositories, but I'm not sure I
have extra-large.

CAROL
(alone, she secretly picks up the phone, dials)
Hello? B18—any messages? . . . Yes . . . Howard . . . what time?
. . . OK. Anything else?
(tense and interested)
Yes? Did he say what number he'd be at? What time? OK,
OK . . .
(She hangs up.)

PHYLLIS
(entering from USL)
I found this Bergdorf's bag, so if you suddenly barf it'll be into
familiar surroundings. Who'd you call?

CAROL
Call?

PHYLLIS
Yes, the second I left the room you dove for the instrument like
you were going down on Cary Grant.

CAROL
Look, I like to check my service because Howard's had a bad
day . . .

PHYLLIS
Can we get back to who my husband left me for?

CAROL
Maybe if I had some coffee.

PHYLLIS
I figured out who it was.

CAROL
It's none of my business.

PHYLLIS
Sure it is—

CAROL
It's not—I'm sorry it happened—my head is swimming.

PHYLLIS
Know who it is?

CAROL
Please, Phyllis.

PHYLLIS
It's you, you bitch!

CAROL
Oh—the arrant paranoia!

PHYLLIS
Don't give me that, toots—he's been dipping his wick in you
for longer than I probably think.

CAROL
You're nuts—get a grip on yourself.

PHYLLIS
You're gonna have to come clean anyhow—if you want to go
off with him. It's a nice little fillip for Howard—first Dad in the
laughing academy and then a Dear John letter from the little
woman.

CAROL
You know, I'm so turned around that I can't even respond to
this well.

PHYLLIS
Have you been having an affair with Sam?

CAROL
No.

PHYLLIS
Just tell me.

CAROL
No.

PHYLLIS
I just want the truth.

CAROL
I have not—you're such a bully.

PHYLLIS
I figured it out, harlot. You've been phoning each other, meeting secretly, traveling together—

CAROL
I won't sit here and be accused—
(She rises but, still woozy, she sits.)

PHYLLIS
Now—*after* the fact—I remember so many obvious things—the looks across the table—the getting lost together on the trip to Normandy. Howard and I looked for two hours—and the night you ate here and Sam went downstairs to put you in a cab—I'm sitting in bed for an hour and a half while he decides to walk you home—you know, as I speak it's occurring to me that three years ago—three fucking years ago—you and Sam were in New York for a week with Howard in L.A. and me at a convention in Philadelphia—that was three years ago, or does it go back even further than that?

CAROL
It's not me!

PHYLLIS
I found his Filofax. You're all over it!

CAROL
(rises, screams and cries)
What do you want me to do? We fell in love! You're such a bully!

PHYLLIS
Chrrrist!

CAROL
Bully! Bully! We fell in love—nobody planned it—nobody wanted to hurt anyone.

PHYLLIS

I knew it—from the night we met the two of you in the Hamptons. I said she's trouble—she's a troubled broad—she reeks from problems—neurosis oozes out of every pore—

CAROL

This affair has caused us nothing but anguish and pain.

PHYLLIS

Not to mention an occasional orgasm.

CAROL

Don't dirty it up—it's not what you think.

PHYLLIS

I said that first night when we drove home—he seems nice— a little lost but decent—but she's borderline and carnivorous.

CAROL

Stop being so judgmental—you know from your work these things happen—it's nature—it's like lightning—two people meet—a spark flares up and suddenly there's a life of its own.

PHYLLIS

You're describing Frankenstein.

CAROL

It's serious, Phyllis.

PHYLLIS

How long has this been going on? Three years? More? Four? Five?

CAROL

Not even three.

PHYLLIS

So, two? Two years you two have been sneaking around town like dogs in heat?

CAROL

We haven't been sneaking around town—we have an apartment.

PHYLLIS

An apartment? Where?

CAROL

The East Fifties—

PHYLLIS

How big?

CAROL

Small—

PHYLLIS

What?

CAROL

Three rooms.

PHYLLIS

Rent-controlled?

CAROL

Stop being snotty—we're trying to communicate—

PHYLLIS

What do you need three rooms for? You entertain?

CAROL

Never. Never. I swear. It's just a place to go to, to be alone—to relax—to—to—to talk—

PHYLLIS

To talk—to exchange ideas. To exchange fluids.

CAROL

We're in love, Phyllis—oh God—I never thought I'd be saying this—it's—everything—yes, it's sensual, but it's more—we share feelings and dreams.

PHYLLIS

Why did I let you into my life—I knew all the time you'd fuck a snake if they held its head.

CAROL

Phyllis, what do you want me to say? He fell out of love with you years ago. I don't know why. Certainly not over me. It was finished in his mind between you two before he ever said anything to me.

PHYLLIS

How did he first do it?

CAROL

Do what?

PHYLLIS

When? What night?

CAROL

What's the difference?

PHYLLIS

You probed—I want answers.

CAROL

New Year's Eve at Lou Stein's party.

PHYLLIS

Oh my God—that was 1990.

CAROL

'91—er, '90, right . . .

PHYLLIS

And what happened? Who groped whom first?

CAROL

That wasn't it. He came over to me—I was watching the fireworks—and he whispered in my ear—can you meet me for lunch next week without mentioning anything to Phyllis. Well, you can imagine, I was a bit surprised.

PHYLLIS

I'm sure. You probably started to lubricate.

CAROL

I said, Why? He said, I need your help on something.

PHYLLIS

And where was I when this adolescent bullshit was going on?

CAROL

You had led a group against their wills out onto the terrace, in the five-degree temperature, to watch the fireworks. And Howard was in the kitchen getting the Steins' recipe for baba ghanoush.

PHYLLIS

Yes—I remember—your husband had just enrolled in a cooking course and we were all so proud of him.

CAROL

And I said, what kind of help? With what? And Sam said, Phyllis's birthday is soon and I want you to help me get her something, but it has to be something special.

PHYLLIS

And it was, folks.

CAROL

So the following Thursday we had lunch at his club and pitched some gift ideas back and forth. And after lunch we went on our shop— I remember going to Bergdorf's and Tiffany's and James Robinson and finally in this tiny old antique store on First Avenue we found a stunning pair of art deco earrings— diamonds with tiny rubies—

PHYLLIS

I know the earrings. I've seen them on you.

CAROL

Well, I was flabbergasted. He bought them, and we walked out on the street and he handed the box to me and said, Here, I want you so badly.

PHYLLIS

And what did you say?

CAROL

I said, Whoa—wait a minute—we came to buy Phyllis a birthday present—if I take this we have to at least pick out *something* for her.

PHYLLIS

Thanks, you're such a doll. So I wound up with those stinking silver candlesticks.

CAROL

They cost a fortune.

PHYLLIS

They're old-lady candlesticks—they're something you'd give
Miss Havisham! And of course you never thought of saying—
Phyllis is your wife and I'm her friend—

CAROL

May I tell you why not?

PHYLLIS

I know why not, you cheap little tart—because you had your
predatory sights set on Sam from the minute you met him.

CAROL

Not so—

PHYLLIS

Don't give me that shit—you met us and took one look at him
and started rubbing your hands together and salivating because
he works for a show business law firm and he's in shape and
has muscles and compared to that shriveled up, emasculated,
goat-turd of a husband you have, Sam has to seem like the
answer to a bovine frump's prayer.

CAROL

He couldn't stand being married to you anymore and he told
me that over lunch—*he* initiated the relationship—*he* salivated
over me—he looked me in the eye at lunch and tears formed—
I'm not happy, he said—

PHYLLIS

Tears formed in Sam's eyes? Was his athletic supporter too
tight?

CAROL

From the first moment Howard and I met you and Sam I knew
he was miserable. This woman is not making him happy—
I told that to Howard that first night we met you—

PHYLLIS

I can see the picture at home—you brushing your former
teeth—Howard slipping into his nightgown and sleeping cap—
discussing your betters—planning your little social climb—

CAROL

She may be a brilliant shrink and the center of every
conversation with some new variation of how great she is—but
she's not enough woman for him—she's not there to guide
him—to bring him coffee—

PHYLLIS

Can you pass me that airsick bag?

CAROL

Sam had tremendous hostility—but you know that now.

PHYLLIS

The thought of you and Sam discussing me over cocktails or
postcoital Marlboros.

CAROL

We tried to break it off several times but we couldn't.

PHYLLIS

I'm sure you tried. But I know Sam—when that old sperm
count rises—you got the phone call—"Beat it over here, honey,
I want to get my rocks off and whine about my wife."

CAROL

It wasn't like that—we spoke more often than made love.

PHYLLIS

About what? Chrrrist! What the hell did he find to talk about
with you? He's a man's man—what the hell did you have to
discuss with him besides me? Your cellulite? Your eye jobs and
face-lifts? Shopping? Your trainer? Your nutritionist? Or did
you just lay on his shoulder and giggle about the ironic shrink
who could see everybody's problems but her own?

CAROL

I did nothing wrong. Your husband stopped loving you before
he met me.

PHYLLIS

Bullshit!

CAROL

And it was obvious to all our friends—

PHYLLIS

They're not *our* friends—they're *my* friends and I brought you
in—like a fool—you met them all through me—

CAROL

And they all knew you and Sam were a joke as a couple—

PHYLLIS

Bullshit.

CAROL

Believe me, I didn't seduce Sam. He played around plenty
before I came on the scene.

PHYLLIS

Like hell!

CAROL

Face up to it!

PHYLLIS
I'm not interested in your fantasies.

CAROL
Ask Edith Moss and Steve Pollack's secretary—

PHYLLIS
Liar! Slut! You're the all-American whore! They should put
your diaphragm in the Smithsonian.

CAROL
Don't lay it all on me! I didn't turn your husband into a
philanderer—

PHYLLIS
Trollop, tart, prostitute—

CAROL
You're such a phony—pretending your marriage is so perfect—
you were a laughingstock—

PHYLLIS
I loved Sam and I was a damn good wife.

CAROL
We happened to fall in love—but before he met me, he was
groping several of your closest high-class friends—including
Madelaine Cohen, who also being a shrink probably dissected
you with far greater insight than I'm capable of.

PHYLLIS
Madelaine Cohen's a strict Freudian complete with beard!
(Door buzzer rings. Phyllis gets it. It's Howard.)

HOWARD
What a day—oh brother—I need a drink.

PHYLLIS
Howard, guess what?

CAROL
Will you keep quiet.

HOWARD
(pouring himself a drink)
You look at them in that home and you realize that's what it all comes to—to that—to that. My God—what's the point of anything if it ends up like that—

PHYLLIS
Carol has some news for you that might cheer you up.

CAROL
Will you stop—she's drunk, Howard.

HOWARD
I mean to get good and drunk tonight. God, Carol—here's my father who was a strapping, virile man—he took me to ball games.

PHYLLIS
Tell him, Carol—he needs a lift.

HOWARD
This poor old lady, ninety-one, used to be a singer—sits at the piano—she's ancient—trying to gasp her way through a chorus of "You're the Cream in My Coffee" . . . the others stare—some perfunctory applause—and these living dead seated in stupors before the communal TV, their clothes stained from food that dribbles all over them . . .

PHYLLIS
I hope you reserved us all a place—

HOWARD
I can't bear it! It's too much to bear!

CAROL
Have your drink—

HOWARD
Two people grow old together—like my mother and father—
we decay—one of us breaks down faster—the other watches—
after years of being together—suddenly you're alone—

PHYLLIS
It may not happen quite that way for you, Howard—

HOWARD
No . . .
(to himself)
It might not.

PHYLLIS
Tell him, Carol—

HOWARD
Tell me what? What's going on? Why are you drunk so early?
And what the hell's all this?
(Noticing the mess for the first time.)

CAROL
Howard, there's something we need to discuss—

HOWARD
What?

CAROL
I'm not sure this is the time or place.

PHYLLIS
Howard, Carol's leaving you.

CAROL
Will you let us be—

HOWARD
I don't get it.

PHYLLIS
She's leaving you—she's going off with another man.

HOWARD
Meaning what?

PHYLLIS
Meaning you're out—no more wifekins—she's been fucking my husband for three years and she's going off with him.

CAROL
(to Phyllis)
You're detestable.

PHYLLIS
Am I lying? Close your mouth, Howard.

HOWARD
Is this true, Carol?

CAROL
Sam and I fell in love—we didn't mean to hurt anybody.

HOWARD
(sitting slowly)
N-no—I'm sure you didn't . . .

PHYLLIS

Jesus, aren't you going to get mad?

HOWARD

What's the point? That won't undo things—

PHYLLIS

There's a time to be rational and a time to run amok—I keep the steak knives in the kitchen.

HOWARD
(not understanding)
You never had a good word to say about Sam.

PHYLLIS

She was deceiving you, Howard.

CAROL

Will you shut up! You hover around making spiteful remarks— things are bad enough.

HOWARD
(simply)
She was always so jealous of you, Phyllis—

PHYLLIS

She's certainly paid me back.

HOWARD

Sam was my friend—

CAROL

Why do you tell her I'm jealous of her? How was I ever jealous?

HOWARD

It was more than jealously. You were obsessed with her.

CAROL

You're dreaming, Howard.

HOWARD

I'm a writer, Carol—I know how to recognize obsession—

CAROL

You're a failed writer, Howard—judging from the characters you create you shouldn't even be a writer—you should be in the cardboard business.

HOWARD

And I say you were obsessed with everything about Phyllis.

CAROL

I was not, goddamn it!

PHYLLIS

Children, let's not quarrel.

HOWARD

Jesus, Carol, you thought she was an artist. You thought of going back to school to study psychiatry.

PHYLLIS

So the truth comes out—hero worship.

CAROL

Stop drinking, Howard, you're worse than me.

HOWARD

I can drink—you're the one who makes a spectacle—she used to dress like you—remember? And you wanted to cut your hair—

PHYLLIS

This is becoming positively morbid.

CAROL

I was always fascinated by psychology. I minored in it at college.

HOWARD

You minored in history.

PHYLLIS

I thought it was art.

CAROL

I was an art history major.

HOWARD

She likes to say she hasn't found herself.

PHYLLIS

Has she tried looking in the reptile house?

CAROL
(explaining rationally)
There was a period of time that I was very impressed by you.

HOWARD

And she talked of becoming a shrink.

PHYLLIS

Fortunately they have licensing laws—

HOWARD

She was going to combine it with her yoga—an Eastern religion psychotherapy. An Eastern religious, holistic, zen, waking dream therapy.

PHYLLIS

How were you going to cure your patients, by dipping them in the Ganges?

CAROL

Go ahead—make fun of me.

HOWARD

And for a while she dressed like you—she ordered all those simple skirts and tops—I remember on more than one occasion you rejected an outfit because you said Phyllis Riggs would never wear anything like that.

CAROL

He makes this up. Howard, your father's dying, don't take it out on me.

HOWARD

Carol's always had an identity problem. She doesn't know who she is. Or rather, she knows who she is and she's desperately trying to find someone else to be—and who can blame her?

CAROL

All right, calm down. I think you're overdue for your treatments. Howard's mood swings are getting worse. He doesn't like it known.

HOWARD

Don't change the subject.

CAROL

That's what I've had to put up with all these years, manic highs and lows. He recently tried joining the Hemlock Society, but they rejected him.

PHYLLIS

Rejected by the Hemlock Society? I'd kill myself.

CAROL

Don't say that—you've never seen him in a gray funk eyeing the plastic bags in the cupboard.

HOWARD
I'm not going to wind up in one of those homes, I'll tell you that.

CAROL
And then just as quickly he'll become happy—too happy.

HOWARD
Quiet, Carol.

CAROL
God, if you think I shop—when Howard swings into his uphill phase—he'll just check into the Plaza and run up all kinds of bills—champagne and caviar and things he'll never wear—and big plans and grandiose schemes—and the only thing that straightens him out is electricity. This man needs his voltage like we need our collagen. And he begs me to hide it.

HOWARD
At least I have an identity. I'm Howard who's manic-depressive. Carol wants to be you, but you're already taken—

PHYLLIS
So she steals my husband.

HOWARD
It's not just you—she identifies with lots of people.

CAROL
I didn't steal your husband—he came after me.

HOWARD
Her real identity crisis was with her art professor at school.

CAROL
Let's drop the subject now. I think we should go home.

HOWARD
Home? We have no more home.

PHYLLIS
What about her college professor?

CAROL
Howard, I'm warning you—

HOWARD
As long as we're coming clean, you may as well know that
when we met, Carol had this art professor—quite a brilliant
woman—not with your honors but very impressive . . .

CAROL
Howard, I will not stay here while you tell this story.

HOWARD
And Carol grew to idolize this professor and identify with her.

CAROL
Quiet! Quiet!

HOWARD
(shaking Carol)
Will you shut up!

CAROL
Don't you dare attack me!

PHYLLIS
Howard, you have a temper. Who would have thought it of a
man who named his goldfish Dorothy?

HOWARD

She identified with Professor Kanin as much as she identified with you—duplicating her wardrobe—braiding her hair, taking on her mannerisms—reflecting all her tastes—and because Professor Kanin had a tiny child, Carol decided she wanted to be a mother.

CAROL

I don't care if you tell this story because I can hold my head high.

HOWARD

And so she begged me to make her pregnant—which I did—

CAROL

With some effort, darling—don't leave out the part about the sudden impotence. Talk about trying to stuff an oyster into a parking meter.

HOWARD

Not that I wanted a child—nor did Carol down deep.

CAROL

You never knew what I felt down deep about anything.

HOWARD

But how else to become Professor Kanin—the idol of the day.

CAROL

You couldn't make me pregnant—is that the story you want to tell? Because that's the long and short of it.

HOWARD

She visited a fertility expert—and every few days I'd be asked to masturbate into a test tube—

PHYLLIS
My God, what an aim you must have had.

HOWARD
So she could run with it in a taxicab and while the sperm were still fresh and squiggling—

CAROL
Yours didn't squiggle, Howard, they wandered aimlessly—

HOWARD
To make a long story short—science worked its magic and she got knocked up. Her dream was going to come true. In nine months she would be just like Professor Kanin—with her Laura Ashley skirts and the Aztec jewelry—art major, mother, the works—she wouldn't have to go on being that unenviable character Carol.

PHYLLIS
I can see this coming—she got cold feet—went to a drunken illegal abortionist who operated on her face by mistake, and that's why she looks the way she looks.

HOWARD
Cold feet is exactly what she got, but in her eighth month. Suddenly she didn't want to be a mother.

CAROL
(softly)
No—I didn't.

HOWARD
Reality set in and she said to herself, Hey, it's one thing to have fantasies of identification—but I'm not Professor Kanin and I don't want a child.

CAROL
Why are you doing this?

HOWARD
To make a long story short she gave birth to an eight-pound
little boy who was quite cute considering he resembled the
movie actor Broderick Crawford—but you know they all look
like old men. I mean, they're bald—and I bonded in the first
few days—but darned if she didn't give him away. She insisted
on placing him out for adoption—

PHYLLIS
And you stood back and let her do it—you were probably very
reasonable and well mannered.

HOWARD
I remember it so clearly—the day we gave him up I thought—
hey, if I take one of those bags that keep sandwiches fresh and
place it over my head wouldn't that be a nice feeling.

PHYLLIS
Well, you make a lovely couple and if there was a special
Academy Award for defective humans you'd have my vote.
And now—I'm going to the toilet and I want both of you out
of here when I return.
(Phyllis exits SL.)

HOWARD
So I guess it's over between us. After all these years.

CAROL
I guess it never should have begun.

HOWARD
Why do you say that, Carol? It certainly began OK—the first
few days went well enough.

CAROL

No—it was my fault. You'd have done better if you had
married that what's her name—Ida—Ida—

HOWARD

Rondilino—

CAROL

Rondilino. I shouldn't have taken you away from her—but I
wanted to be with a creative soul—a writer—

HOWARD

You didn't take me away from Ida. I saw you and I went after
you.

CAROL

That's what you *think*—but the night we all double-dated, and
I decided I wanted to marry you, you were dead meat.

HOWARD

Poor Ida.

CAROL

Ida was insipid. But better suited to you than I am. We
disappointed each other too much.

HOWARD

Did you ever cheat on me prior to your affair with Sam?

CAROL

No—yeah, once. My dentist.

HOWARD

Oh, Carol—

CAROL

Do you know he charged me for an extra filling?

HOWARD
Who else?

CAROL
No one . . . Jay Roland.

HOWARD
My collaborator?

CAROL
Oh, Howard, he was such a bad writer—but sexy with that ponytail.

HOWARD
You slept with my writing partner?

CAROL
Once. You were in the hospital getting shock treatment and we were both so concerned about you and we didn't know how to express it.

HOWARD
Who else?

CAROL
No one—that's it—that's it. Those were the years—fifteen arid years—without ever getting up the nerve to leave—betting wrong that all your mental instability was a sure sign of literary genius when in fact it was just plain dementia.

HOWARD
Where will you live?

CAROL
Sam has talked about London.

HOWARD
I don't want you to leave me, Carol.

CAROL
How can I not, Howard? I've become involved with someone who means something to me—something real—there's feeling—there's passion.

HOWARD
I'm a person who can't be alone, Carol.

CAROL
You'll get by—Howard, try and understand, I'm nearly fifty— how many more chances will I get? Let me go with this guiltlessly.

HOWARD
But I'm scared—

CAROL
I can see this has triggered one of your downswings—this and committing your father to a home. Why don't we call Doctor Carr—maybe it's a good time to go in and get your head zapped.
(She notices that Howard has removed a pistol from his pocket.)
Howard—what are you doing!?

HOWARD
I think life is a black hole.

CAROL
Oh my God! Howard—don't!

HOWARD
It's unbearable! I don't want to live.

CAROL
Where did you get that gun?

HOWARD
This was amongst my father's possessions—he was in the
Great War—I mean, the first Great War—the war to end all
wars—only of course it didn't, people being what they are—

CAROL
Put that down!

HOWARD
It's all so squalid and meaningless!

CAROL
Help! Phyllis! Phyllis!

HOWARD
Shut up, my head's throbbing!

CAROL
Suicide is not the answer!

HOWARD
It all comes to nothing—a void, a home for the aged.

CAROL
Black moods pass! It's just the moment—Phyllis! Goddamn it!
Suicide is not the answer.

HOWARD
I'm frightened!

CAROL
Oh God, I don't want to watch!

HOWARD

You won't have to watch. I'm going to kill you first—then myself.

CAROL

Me? Howard, you're joking!

HOWARD

First you, then me!

CAROL

Help! Help! Phyllis!

HOWARD

If you don't close that yap!
(He pulls back the hammer.)

CAROL

Howard, don't! Don't!

HOWARD

Give me one good reason why we should both live?

CAROL

Because we're human beings, Howard—fallible and often stupid but not evil—not really—just pathetic—mistaken— desperate—

HOWARD

We're alone in the cosmos!

CAROL

Howard—this is not the cosmos—this is Central Park West!

HOWARD

No! It's no use! I want to die!
(Howard points the gun at his own head and pulls the trigger,
but it jams. He points the gun at Carol and pulls the trigger
repeatedly, but it continues to jam.)
Goddamnit! It's old—it's too old—it's broken! It's a German
Luger—it should be like a Mercedes!
(Carol pulls the gun away from Howard.)

CAROL

Give me that! You lunatic! What's the matter with you!?
I'm shaking like a leaf! I'm trembling, I feel faint! I need a
Valium—
(Phyllis enters. She is oblivious to what has been going on.)

PHYLLIS

What's all the noise—I thought I said out.

CAROL

(shaken)
Howard wanted to kill us—both—first me and then himself—
his father's pistol—a souvenir—but—but—but—it jammed—
he pulled the trigger—but—it jammed—
(Phyllis picks up the pistol and fools with it.)

PHYLLIS

There's nothing wrong with this gun, Howard. You forgot to
unlock the safety latch.

CAROL

I'm going to be sick!
(Carol exits. Phyllis sits with Howard on the couch.)

PHYLLIS

The truth is, Howard, that even though you are suffering from
one of your clinical depressions, you are correct to be
depressed. Even a clock that is broken is right twice a day.

Depressing things have happened to you. First you put your
dear, sweet father in a second-rate home for the aged—

HOWARD
It's not second-rate.

PHYLLIS
Face it, Howard, the best of them are none too good, but the
one you chose, sensibly within your budget, is—and you'll
understand this—a schlock house. Following the experience
of parting with a parent, which, by the way, brings you
psychologically one step closer to realization of the end of
your own life—your wife is abandoning you for your good
friend—a successful male with a higher testosterone level—
whom of course she has been diddling for two years behind
your back. So it's almost healthy for you to be depressed. If
you were not depressed, you'd be an idiot. Am I being helpful?

HOWARD
I miss my son . . .

PHYLLIS
I give this whole thing six months.

HOWARD
Sam and Carol? They may move to London.

PHYLLIS
Six months whether it's London or Tierra del Fuego. They're
both too dysfunctional.

HOWARD
I knew he fooled around.

PHYLLIS
Did you?

HOWARD
Who didn't?

PHYLLIS
Just me, I suppose.

HOWARD
I think just you, Phyllis—I even think I heard a dirty innuendo
from a busboy at "21."

PHYLLIS
The busboy knew?

HOWARD
Naturally he didn't know I knew Sam or you, and Sam was
entering and I was having lunch and I saw the busboy nudge
the waiter and nod toward Sam and point to a sexy brunette
and he said, What nerve—he's banging her and yet he comes
in with his wife all the time. I was surprised he knew the term
"banging" because he was just over from Poland.

PHYLLIS
That's a great story, Howard. The waiter and the Polish busboy
knew but not me.
(The front door opens and Sam enters.)

SAM
(coldly firm)
I came to get the rest of my papers—
(seeing his work strewn on floor)
Oh Jesus, what did you do?

PHYLLIS
I need a couple of answers from you, big shot.

SAM

You had your go at me. I tried the reasonable route. I'm not
getting my skull fractured by an hysteric—

HOWARD

You've been carrying on with my wife for two years.

SAM

You I'll talk to, Howard, and I'll start with an apology.

PHYLLIS

That just makes it all OK, doesn't it?

SAM

I said I didn't want to hear from you. I'm here to get my
papers—look what you've done . . .

HOWARD

I can't easily accept your apology, Sam, because we're supposed
to be close.

SAM

(angry at Phyllis as he picks up all his papers from floor)
I have some complicated cases going—

PHYLLIS

So you were screwing all my friends.

SAM

These last couple of years have not been easy for me, Phyllis—
my work has not gone well. Why did you tear up everything?

PHYLLIS

I said, so you were screwing all my friends—

SAM

I wasn't screwing all your friends—

PHYLLIS

Liar! I know—I know everything!

SAM

If you know everything you don't need me to tell you
anything. Get your foot off those papers—get it off—
(forces it off)
Get it off!

PHYLLIS

Ouch—you bastard!

SAM

I gave you a chance to talk things out—I poured my guts out to
you today—and where'd it get me?

PHYLLIS

I trusted you. How am I supposed to know that underneath
you're seething with discontent? If only you had been honest
instead of letting your gripes fester and taking up with my
friends.

HOWARD

(rising pugnaciously)
I'm angry at you, Sam—you made me a cuckold—

SAM

(pushes him down)
Sit down, Howard. We can talk later. I said I apologize.

PHYLLIS

I know you slept with Edith and Helene—what about Polly?

SAM
You're cuckoo. I'm so glad to be out of this.

PHYLLIS
You're not out yet, sugar.

SAM
As soon as I get this mess together, I'm history.

HOWARD
She knows about the brunette at "21"—with the bangs and the full lips.

SAM
Howard, I'm sorry about me and Carol—I honestly didn't think you'd ever find out.

PHYLLIS
(turning on Sam)
What about my sister?

SAM
What?

PHYLLIS
What about Susan?

SAM
What about Susan?

PHYLLIS
Did you sleep with her too?

SAM
You're hallucinating.

PHYLLIS

Hallucinating. That's the word you used to deny Carol when I found the Filofax.

SAM

Because it was absurd.

PHYLLIS

How absurd can it be? If you were sleeping with Carol, why not Susan? Now it all comes back to me. I used to notice you stare at her—and she always went to watch you play softball in East Hampton.

HOWARD

What kind of woman are you, Phyllis, that all these seemingly close people willingly betray you?

PHYLLIS
(stopped by this, regains poise)
You need shock treatment, Howard. Why don't you wet your finger and put it in the socket.

SAM

I'm gathering my papers and I'm out of here. Out—out—for good—forever.

PHYLLIS
(goes to phone)
I'm calling Susan—

SAM

Put that down!
(He takes it from her, hangs up.)

PHYLLIS

Look at the nostrils flare. He's scared.

SAM

Scared of what? I'm finished in your life.

PHYLLIS
(taking phone again)
Hey, lover, a girl can phone her sister, can't she?

SAM

You insist on making a fool of yourself.

PHYLLIS
(dials)
My first husband appreciated women too, but he didn't act
out—may he rest in peace—or Secaucus or wherever the hell
he's living—
(on phone)
Hello, Donald, put Susan on—

SAM

I can't believe she can still rattle me—
(He pours himself a drink.)

HOWARD

She's a ballbuster—but you did some evil things, Sam.

SAM
I did zero.

PHYLLIS
(on phone)
Susan—did you have an affair with Sam? I'm asking you if
you had an affair with Sam? . . . When you stayed here . . .
Well, I don't buy it, Susan! . . . I say you did—I say that was
your way of getting even with me . . .

HOWARD

Even for what? Did you sleep with Susan's husband?

PHYLLIS
(to Howard)
Of course I didn't sleep with Susan's husband.
(on phone)
What?—No, I didn't sleep with Donald! Would I sleep with a
Hasidic jeweler? But you did with Sam! Because you're a
gypsy—a lost soul—and it was my generosity that kept you
afloat and you resented me and this is how you repay me!
(She hangs up angrily.)

SAM
Bravo—now you've made yourself an ass in her eyes because,
baby doll—

PHYLLIS
Don't call me baby doll—

SAM
Because, Godzilla, I never laid a finger on Susan.

HOWARD
Who *was* that brunette at "21."

SAM
Howard, why don't you get some rest?
(Enter Carol, surprised to see Sam.)

CAROL
Sam.

SAM
Hello, Carol.

CAROL
Phyllis and Howard know everything. It's been quite a night.

HOWARD

It's like a boil was lanced and all the pus is coming out.

CAROL

Can we go, Sam? I need an hour to pack at home.

SAM

Go where?

CAROL

To our apartment, to Amagansett, if you want, straight to London—I just don't care anymore.

SAM

I don't understand—where are we going?

CAROL

Out of here—look, we all clearly need new lives—not just Sam and me—but Howard and Phyllis—let's try and look at tonight as a beginning—we don't have to give in to our bleakest thoughts. I know—it sounds easy for me to say because Sam and I have each other—but we can be civilized and help one another get through this.

SAM

Just a minute—we're not going away—

CAROL

Well, you mentioned London—I mean, away is just out of here.

SAM

Carol, I think you misunderstood.

CAROL

What?

SAM

I met someone and I'm in love.

CAROL

What do you mean?

SAM

I met a woman and I'm in love.

CAROL

I don't understand—you're in love with me.

SAM

No—we had a fling but—we never were in love.

CAROL

I am.

SAM

Oh, but—I never—you thought I was leaving Phyllis for you?

CAROL

Sam—

PHYLLIS

Sometimes there's God so quickly.

SAM

Carol—I was crystal clear on that point—at least I thought I
was.

CAROL
(staggering)
Legs—legs—going to faint—the room is spinning—

HOWARD
Get some smelling salts.
(laughing)
Ha, ha, ha . . .

PHYLLIS
(to Carol)
Honey, what *were* you thinking?

CAROL
Sam—Sam—all those afternoons—we talked—

SAM
But that was the whole point—we were both just having a fling.

CAROL
That's how it started—

SAM
And it never changed.

CAROL
Of course it did.

SAM
Of course it didn't.

HOWARD
(amused by it all)
This is truly comical.

CAROL
But all the talk about the future—and London—

SAM
But that was just speculating—there was no actual plan—

CAROL
There was—

SAM
There couldn't have been—we never had that kind of a
relationship.

CAROL
Of course we did—

SAM
We were never in love—at least I wasn't.

CAROL
You told me you were—

SAM
Of course not—you're dreaming—

CAROL
"I've got to end my marriage—I'm suffocating—I'm
drowning—the time with you is the only thing that keeps me
alive—"

SAM
In the context of illicit sex—I told you the ground rules from
day one.

CAROL
Yes—but—it—it—seemed to change—to deepen—you asked
me if I could be happy in London?

SAM
Carol, you're reading into it—

CAROL
(total realization)
You bastard—you used me.

PHYLLIS
(annoyed)
How was I suffocating you? Why were you drowning? Huh?
You clown.

HOWARD
(getting jollier)
He's a clown—this is a circus and he's a clown—and we're all
freaks.

CAROL
You lied to me—you lied to me—

PHYLLIS
You got what you deserved, you crypto-hooker.

CAROL
"I want to be with you, Carol—with you I'm happy—with you
I know my only real moments—rescue me from that self-
centered storm trooper who's crushed my hopes—"

PHYLLIS
A Nazi? Did you tell her I was a Nazi?

SAM
(innocently)
I never said you were an actual party member.

CAROL
I don't believe this! You can't make love like that without
feeling love.

PHYLLIS
A stiff prick knows no conscience.

CAROL
(shattered)
This was real—this was true . . .

SAM
(turning on Carol)
Don't hold me responsible for your wishful thinking! I was
aboveboard down the line.

CAROL
No—

PHYLLIS
A woman with a tenuous grasp of reality . . .

CAROL
You're the one with no grasp of reality. Deluded into thinking
you had your marriage under control while he's off with
everybody.

SAM
That's enough, Carol.

CAROL
In your own bed with Nancy Rice.

PHYLLIS
Nancy Rice is on the ethics committee!

SAM
(to Carol)
What good does it do to provoke?

PHYLLIS

Nancy Rice is chairwoman of the ethics committee at the hospital—her specialty is moral choice.

SAM

Yes, I had a quick moment with Nancy Rice when you were in Denver, but she instigated it. And you and I had no more sex life to speak of.

PHYLLIS

Now I know why we didn't—a man cannot ejaculate every day in double figures.

SAM

That's not the reason!

PHYLLIS

No? What's the reason?

SAM

What's the reason? What are we yelling for?

PHYLLIS

What's the reason our lovemaking disappeared like vapor?

SAM

You want to know the reason?

PHYLLIS

Yes—yes—the reason. Tell me the goddamn reason.

SAM

The spontaneity went out of it.

PHYLLIS

You think you're talking to a retard? I'm not her.
(Meaning Carol.)

HOWARD

One thing Carol is not, is retarded. She has a learning disability, but that's different.

CAROL

Will you shut up, Howard.

HOWARD

Hey—back off—I was explaining why you might *seem* retarded but aren't.

CAROL

He turned off you because you don't care enough to please a man sexually. Am I lying, Sam? Did you not use the term "nude catatonic"?

SAM

Mind your business.

HOWARD

I think the problem is Phyllis can be castrating.

SAM

Will you get back in the woodwork.

HOWARD

You told me as much, Sam. When you get drunk over lunch you babble—where did the time go? What happened to all my promises? Should I feel like Mr. Phyllis Riggs?

PHYLLIS

What madness is this? I'm penalized by everyone because I'm a success? My sister, my friends, my husband—

HOWARD

People never hate you for your weaknesses—they hate you for your strengths.

CAROL

Sam, you led me on—you said you loved me.

SAM

Never—never—

CAROL

Yes—

SAM

I was careful never to use that word.

PHYLLIS

Never fuck a lawyer, they get you on the terminology.

HOWARD

Can we put on some music?

CAROL

Chrrrist! That's always the start of an uphill swing.

HOWARD

I can beat Sam in racquetball.

SAM

Sure you can, Howard.

HOWARD

(putting on music)

It drives him crazy—he's muscular but not coordinated!

SAM

Uh-huh.

CAROL

Sam, I had everything planned—you were going to leave
Phyllis.

HOWARD
He did, Carol, aren't you paying attention?

CAROL
Shut up, you manic psychotic!

HOWARD
Everyone's so down—
(He turns up the music.)

CAROL
Turn that off!

HOWARD
What?

CAROL
Turn it off! Off! Stop!
(Sam turns off the music.)

HOWARD
What's gotten into everybody—you'd think there was a
funeral.

SAM
Howard, calm down.

HOWARD
Everyone's so cranky—probably 'cause you're hungry—why
don't I whip up something?

CAROL
Idiot!

HOWARD
What?

CAROL
Idiot! Fool!

HOWARD
Baba ghanoush! It's perfect!
(Howard exits SR into kitchen.)

CAROL
I cared for you, Sam—I loved you—do love you—

SAM
I didn't mean to lead you on—I tried to be careful—I'm not out
to hurt anybody.
(The doorbell rings—Carol, nearest to the door, opens it,
admitting a very young, beautiful, sexy woman named Juliet
Powell.)

JULIET
(to Sam)
I was waiting downstairs and I got worried—I know you
almost had your head bashed in before and I—when you didn't
come down—

PHYLLIS
No—no—no.

CAROL
Is this her?

JULIET
I debated coming up but you said five minutes—

SAM
This is her—she—Juliet Powell—Carol—Phyllis—well, Dr.
Riggs needs no introduction—

PHYLLIS

No introduction. Just drive me to Bellevue and check me in.

CAROL

You know each other?

SAM

Look—let's lay this all on the line and try to wrap it up with no bullshit. Juliet is—was—a patient of Phyllis's, OK?

PHYLLIS

When did you—?

SAM

(to Carol)

Once a long time ago I happened to notice her in the waiting room—I have my own private access, but every once in a blue moon I glimpse one of Phyllis's wounded either coming or going, in tears or just sitting reading *Town and Country*. And I remember thinking, My God—what a lovely creature— so young and fresh—what problems can she possibly have at her age? And then, as fate would have it, several weeks ago I left the apartment at the same time Juliet emerged from the elevator to enter for her session—and I spoke to her—just hello—but knowing she'd be coming down in fifty minutes— I bought a paper and sat on the park bench across the street and sure enough—fifty-two minutes later on the dot she emerged and I said hello again—what a surprise—and now I'm going to marry her.

PHYLLIS

(to Juliet)

And I'm going to stop being a shrink and join the Hemlock Society.

JULIET
(*ingenuously*)
That's why I quit treatment. I didn't think it was realistic to
continue my analysis with you while I was . . .

PHYLLIS
Fucking my husband? Thank you, Miss Teenage America.

CAROL
Sam, she could be your daughter.

SAM
But she's not. She's the daughter of Mr. and Mrs. Morton
Powell who I don't know from a hole in the wall. Unless you
read *The Wall Street Journal.*

CAROL
But what can you possibly have in common?

SAM
You'd be surprised. This is a charming, educated, twenty-five-
year-old—

JULIET
Twenty-one—

SAM
Well, soon to be twenty-five—four years goes like that—

CAROL
What is it that you do, Miss Powell?

JULIET
Do?

CAROL
Your—line of work . . .

JULIET
Film editor. I mean, I will be when I graduate.

CAROL
Will you be going to the prom?

JULIET
I should have graduated already, but I took a year's hiatus.

PHYLLIS
Miss Powell has had some severe emotional problems.

JULIET
Yes, well—

PHYLLIS
She came to me a year ago—introverted, confused, anorexic—
petrified of men. My goal was to liberate her so she could
emerge as a woman and function.

JULIET
Yes and you did it.

PHYLLIS
Yes, I noticed.

JULIET
It's terrible because I hate to lose you as an analyst. On the
other hand, you always tried to guide me to act in my own best
interests.

PHYLLIS
And you think my fifty-year-old husband is in your best
interests?

JULIET

Well, at first I did have some uncomfortable dreams—the spider dream again—only this time, *you* were the black widow, my mother was the scorpion, and—Carol was the tarantula.

CAROL

You didn't even know me.

JULIET

Sam told me about you and the way he described you—

CAROL

A tarantula—

JULIET

My unconscious formed the spider image from hairy and grasping.

CAROL

Hairy and grasping?

JULIET

But in answer to your question—yes—I had reservations—but Sam described a long-dead marriage and I didn't seem to be coming between anybody—I mean he was already sleeping with Carol and Mrs. Bucksbaum.

PHYLLIS

Who?

JULIET

Mrs. Bucksbaum? The lady on two?

PHYLLIS

Oh, Sam—she's crippled!

SAM

What does that mean? For chrissake, Phyllis—I understand it was not noble of me to cheat but not because the woman has a short leg.

PHYLLIS

How did you do it with her? Did you stand her on a box?

CAROL

(to Sam)

Why am I hairy and grasping? How have I grasped? I gave myself—I gave and I gave—I ran when you called—I broke appointments—I told lies—I juggled my schedule to accommodate and demanded nothing—how could you give her the impression I was a tarantula?

SAM

I'm responsible for what she dreams about you?

CAROL

Do you realize the kind of man you're going to marry?

JULIET

Well, actually marriage is more Sam's idea—I'm content to just see how things go.

SAM

No—I want the commitment—I need it—I can't go on like this—I want something stable for once—I have to bring some sanity to my life. Juliet, you're everything I ever dreamed of.

CAROL

A twenty-year-old anorexic?!

SAM

Twenty-one—and she's a film editor.

PHYLLIS

Six months ago she couldn't look a man in the eye without getting shingles.

SAM

Look, I know what you're all thinking, but this is the real thing. Despite what you two might say—I'm finished as a Don Juan. Promiscuity is no answer. Do you think a person is fulfilled by empty, cheap, stupid adultery?

CAROL

Thanks, Sam, it was meaningful to me too.

SAM
(to Juliet)
All I'm trying to say is I found you and I want this to be forever.

PHYLLIS

What about when she's my age? You'll be gumming your food on Medicare.

CAROL

I know I'm not young and beautiful, but this is too much to take—it's more than I can handle.

HOWARD
(popping in)
I decided to make ravioli—it's the only thing you have—

CAROL

My life is a shambles—

HOWARD

Too bad there's no pesto—but I can do a cream sauce and I'll do small tossed salads with anchovies and balsamic vinegar— who's this?

JULIET
(shaking hands with him)
I'm Juliet Powell.

HOWARD
I'm Howard.

JULIET
See, six months ago I couldn't have just introduced myself.

SAM
Tell me that you're not wavering on our marriage. I need the reassurance.

JULIET
I just want us to be sure, that's all. Why isn't it enough if we keep seeing each other and see where it takes us?

SAM
You're reneging. I thought we'd settled it. Last night you felt certain.

HOWARD
(to Juliet)
What do you want to get married for? You're a kid.

SAM
Howard—

HOWARD
No, I'm serious—she's a kid and you're ancient—ancient, I don't mean ancient but much too old for her.

SAM
That's our business.

HOWARD

And you come to her with such baggage—all those scars and bitterness—fixed in your ways.

SAM

I'm not bitter, Howard, I just want to start over.

HOWARD

Hey, who wouldn't?
(to Juliet)
Marriage is a huge step for anyone—much less a kid like you and a screwed up middle-aged Casanova.

JULIET

I keep telling him I think we should wait.

SAM

I want you.

HOWARD

He's nervous because he knows you'll meet somebody else.

SAM

Will you butt out—this man is certifiable.

HOWARD

Not so fast. I hear what this young woman is saying—you're pushing too hard.
(to Juliet)
What do you need marriage for anyhow? You don't want to lock yourself in with any one guy—you should be out tasting life—you're only a kid once.

JULIET

The truth is I'm just coming out of my shell, thanks to Phyllis.

PHYLLIS
If it's thanks to me, *I'm* signing up for shock therapy. And stop calling me Phyllis—I'm still Dr. Riggs.

CAROL
(running to Sam, hitting him)
I'm a spider?! I'm a hairy, grasping spider?!

SAM
Carol, get off my back.

HOWARD
All I'm saying is she should not be thinking of marriage and especially to you. Remember, Juliet—marriage is the death of hope.

JULIET
The death of hope—what a poetic way to put it.

HOWARD
Actually, I'm a writer.

SAM
(to Howard)
For you it was the death of hope—for us it's a bright future.

JULIET
He brought up marriage—I just got confused.

HOWARD
Juliet, may I call you Juliet?—if this guy's talking lifetime commitment, take my advice and run for your life—your young life—after all, you're so pretty and so appetizing— so luscious and succulent—

PHYLLIS
For chrissake, Howard, you sound like you want to cook her.

SAM
Why are you giving him a shred of credibility? He's a cartoon.

JULIET
I told you, Sam, I've never had an affair before—

HOWARD
Many men will fall in love with you—you're very lovely—
I could and we just met.

SAM
He's competing with me—I can't believe it—he's competing.

HOWARD
What do you plan to do with your life?

JULIET
I'd like to be a film editor.

HOWARD
Hey—perfect for me! You know, I've written a number of
screenplays.

SAM
None that ever sold—oh and a novel.

JULIET
(impressed)
You wrote a novel? How wonderful.

SAM
(losing it a little)
Instantly remaindered. A thinly disguised novel about an ex-
college athlete who's competitive with a brilliant, foul-mouthed
wife who heads the department of a hospital and writes books
and is the center of attention wherever they go and who never
realizes he's weak and she is inadvertently emasculating the
poor bastard so all he lives for is illicit sex.

PHYLLIS
With the physically and mentally handicapped.

HOWARD
Juliet, I have a number of wonderful possibilities on the coast—
actually I expect a call tomorrow from Paramount—

SAM
He's delusional, Juliet—he's got nothing—he *is* nothing.

JULIET
I think I feel a migraine coming on—

SAM
This is incredible. What started out as a minor annoyance has
snowballed into a catastrophe. I love you, Juliet. We vowed it
would be forever—now, let's go.

HOWARD
No so fast, Sam. Juliet and I have real potential.

SAM
He's nuts—he's an emotional yo-yo. In ten minutes we'll be
pulling him in off the window ledge.

HOWARD
Think about California with me. All I have to do is say yes to a
very big deal at MGM.

JULIET
Didn't you say Paramount?

HOWARD
(talking very fast)
I have a great notion for a film, although once you have a
hit they press you for a three-picture deal. I have some high
concept ideas—one I'd like to direct. There's always been quite
a bit of interest in me as a director, but I've always said no. Still,
I might consider it—provided they sweeten the pot. You can do
the editing. I'll wire my real estate broker in Beverly Hills and
we'll rent a house, it's silly to buy at first—you never know
how long you're staying—of course we'll get something
spacious—maybe in Bel Air—I'd love an Olympic-size
swimming pool—it'll be fun for the kids—actually I think I
read that Warren Beatty might be selling his home. Warren's
a very dear friend of mine. Not that we've spent a lot of time
together, but we met at a political rally—
(looks at watch)
Why don't I call him—let's see, it's three hours earlier there—

SAM
(has had enough—he grabs Juliet)
Come on, we're getting out of here.

HOWARD
(stops him)
Hey—not so fast.

SAM
Get out of the way, Howard.

HOWARD
No, Sam—you can't always have your way.

SAM
I said we're going.

JULIET
Now, just a minute here—I'm feeling anxious—

SAM
I'm not waiting—we can discuss it in the car.

HOWARD
Leave her alone.

SAM
Howard . . .

HOWARD
I mean it, Sam, I will not let this girl be pushed around. I mean
to spend the rest of my life with her.

SAM
I said out of my way!
(Sam pushes Howard and a scuffle ensues. The scuffle grows
more and more serious, to everyone's surprise.)

PHYLLIS
All right—knock it off—we're not in the jungle—this is
Central Park West.

JULIET
Stop it—leave him alone!

HOWARD
You're strangling me—

PHYLLIS
Stop it—

JULIET
Please—I can't stand it! Stop!—Stop!—Stop!
(There is a general ad-lib as everyone objects and tries to stop Sam. Juliet picks up the gun and shoots Sam. Screams.)

SAM
Oh my God!

PHYLLIS
Sam!

JULIET
What happened!? It went off!

SAM
I have a terrific pain in my backside.

PHYLLIS
Get an ambulance—

JULIET
I didn't mean to—

PHYLLIS
(to Carol)
Call an ambulance!

JULIET
Everything went red—

CAROL
She's only a kid, but she knew enough to unlock the safety latch. Bravo.

PHYLLIS

Get out of here now—before the police come—just walk out the door calmly and go home.

JULIET

I'm awfully sorry, Sam.

SAM

What is a German Luger doing on my living room table?!

HOWARD

How do you like your ravioli? And does anyone want salad?

PHYLLIS
(to Juliet)
Go—the police will come—they'll see that you're the pretty daughter of a known Wall Street banker and they'll lick their lips and phone the press—

JULIET

I didn't mean it—it was an accident.

PHYLLIS

There are no accidents, baby. You still need me to tell you that? Now go home and stay home. We'll discuss this Monday.
(to Carol)
Give me that!

CAROL

Get your coat, Howard. We're going home. The Movie Channel is showing *The Island of Lost Souls*. I want to see if our names come up.

HOWARD

Can we stop at Zabar's—I'm out of nutmeg.

CAROL
You got enough nutmeg to last a lifetime.

JULIET
Good-bye, Dr. Riggs. See you Monday at our usual time—

SAM
Juliet—Juliet—don't go—I love you—
(As lights fade.)

PHYLLIS
Grow up, Sam—she shot you in the ass—it's called rejection!

ABOUT THE AUTHOR

WOODY ALLEN is a writer, director, and—
sometimes—star of more than twenty
films, including *Annie Hall*. Random
House has also published three of his
side-splitting collections: *Getting Even*,
Without Feathers, and *Side Effects*.
Mr. Allen lives in New York City.

ABOUT THE TYPE

This book was set in Aldus, a typeface created by the German typographer Hermann Zapf in 1954 for the Stempel foundry. Aldus was designed as a companion to Zapf's Palatino typefaces. Palatino was originally designed as a display typeface but also became popular as a text face. Believing Palatino was too bold for text, Zapf designed Aldus at a lighter weight, more suitable for text setting. The typeface is named for the fifteenth-century Italian printer and publisher Aldus Manutius.